Louis Stein

SAN DIEGO COUNTY PLACE-NAMES

SAN DIEGO COUNTY PLACE-NAMES

. . . yesterday's people
. . . today's geography

Lou Stein

Rand Editions — Tofua Press

Published in the United States of America

by Rand Editions/Tofua Press
P.O. Box 2610
Leucadia, California 92024

Second edition, 1978   Fourth printing, 1983
Third printing, 1980   Fifth printing, 1988

Acknowledgments

The quotation on page xv, from *Land in California* by W.W. Robinson, is reprinted by permission of the University of California Press. Copyright © 1948 by W.W. Robinson.

The quotations on pages 44, 75, and 138, from *California Place Names,* Second Edition, revised, by Erwin G. Gudde, are reprinted by permission of the University of California Press. Copyright © 1960 by the Regents of the University of California.

The quotation on pages 129-130, from George R. Stewart's *Names on the Land,* is reprinted by permission of Houghton Mifflin Company.

Tofua Press gratefully acknowledges the map, published by the United States Geological Survey, reproduced on the cover of SAN DIEGO COUNTY PLACE-NAMES.

The San Diego Union is frequently quoted herein; its contribution to this book is appreciated.

Cover and Design   Diane Polster
Editor   Elizabeth Rand

For Ellie, Martha, Paul, and Tanya

*There is no part of the world
where nomenclature is so rich,
humorous, and picturesque as
in the United States of America.
The names of the states and
territories themselves form a
chorus of sweet and most
romantic vocables.*

Robert Louis Stevenson

Foreword

To be a researcher is to walk often in the footprints of earlier scholars. Without the first important place-name studies of John Davidson, Winifred Davidson, and Lena B. Hunzicker, this present compilation of county place-names would have required at least five years of effort on my part instead of my three years of work. The earlier extensive research of John Davidson, particularly, got me off to a running start.

My purpose in this onomastic handbook of San Diego County is to record and preserve the history of most of its existing place-names. The study of a county's place-names is a way of seeing the district's history through a microscope rather than through a telescope. Thereby the names on a county map may come to life as a permanent record of earlier personalities and events, and of geographical descriptions, that academically written histories generally do not include.

The approximately 800 county names herein are largely in current use, of importance, or of special interest. Obsolete and vanished place-names of earlier settlements are not included. Also not included are the place-names of neighborhoods, subdivisions, state or county beaches and parks, monuments, city streets, and highways.

It is a great disappointment that the passage of time has obliterated many early Indian place-names, and the meanings of some existing Indian name-designations. Had a book of this type been attempted 25 or 30 years ago when many nineteenth-century Indians and homesteaders were still alive in our county, much more information of Indian place-namings would have been preserved.

Place-names often disclose activities, aspirations, honorings, special experiences, or conditions of people creating a new way of life. Behind the map-presence of these place-names are stories that mirror the nature of the county's geography and reflect the personal history of many of its settlers. Information regarding the foregoing was obtained from manuscripts, maps, diaries, notebooks, earlier newspapers and magazines, county histories, and many interviews with old-time county residents. All these have contributed to this book's compilation of existing county place-names — and thereby have helped make this an informal and casual "reader" of yesterday's people and today's geography.

I am especially grateful for the patience and re-sourcefulness of Sylvia Arden, Serra Museum librarian. The San Diego Historical Society was most helpful in granting me permission to use their monthly bulletins in my search for county place-name information. Librarians Rhoda Kruse and Don Silva of the California Room, San Diego Public Library, were always keenly interested and helpful, whenever I requested research assistance. Wayne Fabert, Serra Museum, made pertinent valuable suggestions.

My interviews with long-time county residents were a series of experiences I shall never forget. It was also a great pleasure to receive letters with county information from many long-time San Diegans. Eleven county newspapers publicized my search for information regarding earlier people and places. County postmasters, state and county park ranger stations, local chambers of commerce, county historical societies — all these suggested names and addresses of long-time residents in their districts who might supply information for this book.

Eleanor Stein's editing and preparation of the manuscript are especially appreciated.

Manifestly, this compilation is not a definitive work — only a beginning. I hope this book will encourage further research and study. Perhaps a county historical society or a curious graduate student will be motivated to fill in some existing gaps in order to further record and preserve a special aspect of county history hitherto undisclosed.

It is entirely possible for a work of this nature to contain errors, or to omit important entries. I sincerely welcome corrections and additions.

Lou Stein
August 1975

Contents

*The story of California can be
told in terms of its land. Better
still, it can be told in terms of
men and women claiming the
land. These men and women
form a procession that begins
in history and comes down to
the present moment.*
W.W. Robinson,
Land in California

Introduction

Almost daily we use — or hear mention of — places in San
Diego County. Probably we give little thought to their
origin or meaning — and yet there are times when a
place-name piques our curiosity, and we cannot discover its
meaning and history.

Thus it seems reasonable to assume that a pertinent
aspect of local history remains unrevealed, chiefly because
insufficient information has been gathered concerning the
origin and meaning of these place-names in the county.

This book attempts to fill that need, and to afford the
prospect for a new look at San Diego County as may be
revealed through its existing place-names.

This research contains approximately 800 San Diego
County name-designations that fall into the following three
general categories:

1. Some San Diego County place-names are geographic or natural designations.

Indian designations usually described a geographical feature at the sites where Indians lived. Examples are PALA (place of water); POWAY (place where the valley ends); CUYAMACA (place of great rainfall); JAMUL (place of small squashes); IN-KO-PAH (place of mountain people); and CUYAPAIPA (place of a leaning rock).

Spanish descriptive designations of geographical features include AGUA CALIENTE (hot water); PULGAS (fleas) CANYON; DOS CABEZOS (place of two rock heads); ENCINITAS (place of little oaks); and AGUA HEDIONDA (stinking water) CREEK. Yankee descriptive "name fossils" of geographical features include ROUND MOUNTAIN, BOTTLE PEAK, BORREGO BADLANDS, and SEVENTEEN PALMS OASIS.

Some descriptive designations in the county are reminders of flora and fauna once abundant but now greatly reduced in quantity: LOS TULES (reed grass), OAT HILLS, CARRIZO (canebrake) CANYON, GRAPEVINE SPRINGS, BEAR VALLEY, COYOTE CREEK, DEER CANYON, and BORREGO (big-horn sheep) MOUNTAIN.

2. Some San Diego place-names are reminders of yesterday's people.

A few place-names recall earlier military heroes: FORT ROSECRANS (a general), LYONS PEAK (a general), and SWEENEY PASS (a lieutenant). Other places are reminders of pioneers and homesteaders who were outstanding personalities in their locales: BIRCH HILL, named for two "greenhorn" British homesteaders; McCAIN VALLEY, homesteaded by a crusty but lovable cowboy; WARNER SPRINGS, a reminder that Col. Jonathan Warner was the desert equivalent of the famous settler Colonel John Sutter who founded the New Helvetia colony near Sacramento; and ROSE CANYON, named for a shrewd businessman and prominent promoter of San Diego City. Other place-names recall the nostalgia some settlers felt for the locales they left behind: BOSTONIA, ARKANSAS CANYON, ALPINE, CARDIFF, CHIHUAHUA CANYON, and MONSERATE MOUNTAIN.

Many of yesterday's people in the county were plain and earthy in their manner of life. Their occasional folk-type namings reflect a singular simplicity and gusto of designation: MONKEY HILL, HELLHOLE CANYON, MOTHER GRUNDY PEAK, SPOOK CANYON, DOG SPRING, HORSETHIEF CANYON, SOURDOUGH SPRING, BONEYARD CANYON, and JACKASS FLAT.

3. Some San Diego County place-names disclose human interest stories.

The Indian name GUATAY represents an old Indian legend of superstition; DOANE VALLEY is an appellation of tribute to a picturesque Yankee poet and homesteader of that name; RAINBOW was the name of a settler who had the choice of residing in his barn or resigning from his elected post; a romantic twist of matrimony is responsible for the place-naming of SANTEE; a shocking event created the name of TRAGEDY SPRING; an unexpected human event during the Anza march through Borrego Desert bestowed the place-name of SALVADOR CANYON; FALLBROOK was place-named for a successful local farm product; LEUCADIA, OLIVENHAIN, and SAN YSIDRO were idealistic chapters in California's history of earlier colony dwellers; and the town of RAMONA was place-named by default.

Name, though it seem but a
superficial and outward matter,
yet it carrieth much impression
and enchantment.

Francis Bacon

ADOBE SPRINGS. (Spanish for "sun-dried brick.") This descriptive place-name probably derives from the composition of the soil here or from the earlier existence of a nearby adobe structure. (Located east from Oak Grove.)

AGRA. (Latin for "field.") Originally Agra was a railroad cattle loading station on the Santa Margarita Rancho. It is possible its name was designated by an educated railroad supervisor with a classical flair in order to describe the station's location in open country. However, another researcher reports it as a transferred or borrowed name for the Taj Mahal city of Agra in India. (J.D., Ha.)

AGUA CALIENTE: Creek, Hot Springs. (Spanish for "hot or warm water.") The Indian *rancheria* (village) here was between the creek and the hot springs, and its Indian name was "Jacopin" (meaning unknown). In the 1820s the padres from San Diego Mission designated this site as El Agua Caliente. By 1840 a land grant for this site was titled "Valle de San Jose y Agua Caliente." The pioneering in 1844 of Connecticut Yankee Jonathan Trumbull Warner eventually transformed these springs into a famous desert health attraction.

1

In 1847 the Mormon battalion rested here on its march to San Diego. Mormon Sgt. Tyler officially recorded:

> Strange as it may appear, it was asserted not only by Warner but by eyewitnesses of our own men that on cold nights the Indians, who were nearly nude, slept with their bodies in the warm stream, while their heads lay on the soddy banks.

Another Agua Caliente Springs is located in Vallecitos Valley about 35 miles south from Warner Springs. A popular state park now exists here. (J.D., Hu.)

The tautology of Agua Caliente Hot Springs is noteworthy. (See also under WARNER SPRINGS.)

AGUA HEDIONDA: Creek, Lagoon, Rancho. (Spanish for "stinking water.") This descriptive place-name designated the unpleasant odor of a sulphur spring located below Carlsbad; the name soon applied to the district adjacent to the creek and lagoon.

In 1842 a Mexican land grant established Agua Hedionda Rancho, taking its name from the creek. Captain Maria Marron, retired sea officer, received this grant.

Marron was reported to have referred to his rancho as "Rancho San Francisco" in his will. This suggests a displeasure with the "stinking water" nickname. Further: San Francisco Peak was located on Marron's property, and thereby implies a connection between the mountain and the captain's preference for this place-name. *(History of Carlsbad,* published by Friends of the Library of Carlsbad, California.)

Years and years later movie star Leo Carrillo purchased the ranch, remodeling its main structure into an attractive hacienda. At the lagoon is a generating plant erected by the San Diego Gas and Electric Company. Apparently the company evaded the "stinking water" designation by selecting "Encina Plant" as a descriptive place-name for this facility; *Encina* translates as "oak" (which at that time was not to be found in this immediate vicinity!).

The early Californios often applied "Agua Hedionda" up and down California for ponds or springs with unpleasant odors. When the Yankees came they sometimes changed this name to "Sulphur Springs" and in a few locations thereby enriched themselves by developing them as "health" waters. (P. Rush, p. 89 ff.)

AGUA TIBIA: Creek, Mountains. (Spanish for "place of tepid water.") Its Indian name, "Malamai," remains unexplained. A warm spring at the foot of the mountain was used by the Indians for healing purposes. (J.D.) (Located east and north from Pala.)

Throughout California "agua" was a name often applied to surface (spring) waters, the generic often being combined with *fria* (cold), *buena* (good), *tibia* (tepid), *mansa* (quiet), *dulce* (sweet), *mala* (bad), *hedionda* (stinking), and *amargosa* (bitter).

Historical fountain-of-health memo: *The San Diego County Advertiser,* July 30, 1891, editorially exulted:
No section of California is more endowed with restorative and health-giving mineral springs than San Diego County. There are several hundred of these, found in nearly every part of the county − north, south, east, west − in the mountains, plains, valleys, and on the coast. They are of every variety − hot or cold − sulphuretted, chalybeate, carbonated, and alkaline, with various combinations of Nature's chemistry.

AGUANGA MOUNTAIN. This Indian name appeared with several spellings throughout the nineteenth century, and it probably should have been spelled "Awanga." Its meaning remains uncertain: one source reported it to mean "place of the coyote or dog" while another source declared it to mean "place of the falling water." The lands of the Aguanga tribe must have been extensive in its day: Aguanga Mountain lies in San Diego County, northeast from Palomar Mountain, while the remains of the tribe's reservation are now located in Riverside County.(J.D.,G.)

ALISO CANYON. (Spanish for "alder tree.") Fur trappers, surveyors, Yankee pioneers, and travelers often welcomed the sight of alders, for such trees usually were a landmark of the presence of a permanent water supply. Manifestly, such a landmark feature also must have been attractive to the earlier Spanish and Mexican colonists.

The numerous "aliso" and "alder" place-names in this state are testimony of the abundance of these trees (the Yankees from the East often called them "sycamores"). Researcher Gudde reports that the Spanish name-form outnumbered the English name-form in southern California. (G.)

Aliso Canyon is located north from Oceanside.

ALMA CREEK. Probably named after the Alma mine that once was operated in this region of Ocotillo Wells.

ALPINE. This mountain town was established in 1883 by B.R. Arnold, a Connecticut Yankee importer of ivory for piano and organ keys. He came to this district seeking relief from severe asthma — and found it. Mr. Arnold established a store, town hall, library, and cemetery. Honey was the chief product soon after the settlement began.

The naming of this town was reported in *The San Diego Union,* January 1, 1894:

> This suggestive name of Alpine was given to the place by an old lady whose childhood has been passed amid the glorious scenes in Switzerland. To her the changing lights on mountainside and valley, and the exquisitely tinted shadows on distant peaks recalled the similar glories of that other Alpine.

4

The settlement is situated on an old Indian trail that later became a stage coach route between San Diego and Imperial Valley. Ample evidence indicates that this region long ago was a locale of considerable Indian activity. (Ha., J.D., W.D.)

Back county boom notice:

> One of the inducements to settlers in Alpine is the climate, which for pulmonary complaints is not surpassed. . . .Good land ranges from $7.50 to $25 an acre. Many settlers located here during 1891. Fruits and vegetables of all kinds are raised here, not for export, but each family supplying its own needs." *(San Diego County Advertiser,* January 7, 1892.)

ANAHUAC SPRING. The meaning of this Indian place-name is uncertain, variously reported as "water grass," "everlasting waters," "my spring," or "my water." Mission archives recorded this name as "Inaja." Some pioneers in the district were reported to have pronounced the name as "In-yah-ha." It seems likely the above variations may have been largely the result of white man's mispronunciations. (J.D.) (Located west from Cuyamaca Reservoir.)

ANGELINA SPRING. In the 1880s this was known as "Canebrake Spring." Its change to a personal name-form remains unexplained. (See also under CANEBRAKE.) (Located south from Ranchita.)

ANGEL MOUNTAIN. This is a personal place-name rather than a descriptive one: "Angel" was the family name of early homesteaders at this site in the Lake Henshaw district.

ANTONE CANYON. The origin of this apparent personal place-name, located north from La Posta, remains unknown.

"Canyon" was introduced into the Southwest by the early trappers. It was a Spanish term (cañon) for a pipe or cannon. Mexican usage changed it to mean a narrow watercourse among mountains.

ANZA DESERT STATE PARK. Named to honor Juan Bautista de Anza who led the historic Spanish expedition through this district in 1774.

ARKANSAS CANYON. This is a borrowed or transfer place-name: an early settler from Arkansas located here in the 1870s and named the place after his home state. The unfortunate pioneer was murdered on his premises under mysterious circumstances. (Hu., B.) (Located north from Julian.)

ARROYO SALADA. (Spanish for "salty place.") A name-description for a saline watering site in Anza-Borrego Desert.

In Spanish days "arroyo" referred to a watercourse. Often "seco" was added to describe the arroyo's dry condition. "Arroyo" later became a type of generic name in the southwest, and it was sometimes applied to describe either a canyon or a creek.

ARROYO SECO DEL DIABLO. (Spanish for "dry canyon of the devil.") This common type of folk place-name designated an evil or foreboding locale to be avoided. (Located southeast from Agua Caliente Hot Springs.)

ARROYO TAPIADO. (Spanish for "adobe canyon wall.") This place-name describes a canyon with mud-like slopes located in Anza-Borrego Desert.

BALLAST POINT. A small tongue of land extending into San Diego Bay from the eastern coast of Point Loma peninsula. It is shown on Vizcaino's map as "La Punta de los Guijarros" (Spanish for "the place of rounded single stones"). San Diego tradition has it that Yankee sailors used stones from the point as ballast for Boston-bound ships sailing from San Diego. Tradition also relates that some of these "guijarros" later were used as paving stones in several Boston streets. (W.D.)

It is noteworthy that the place-name of the point, like its stones, also had its own historical transfer from Spanish to Yankee.

BALLENA: Town, Mountain, Valley. (Spanish for "whale.") A descriptive place-name designated by early valley settlers who saw this mountain as a whale's outline. This enduring name artifact is a pertinent reminder of the prominence and extent of the whaling industry in the Pacific Ocean. At one time in Spanish conquest Spanish seamen frequently and casually referred to the lower southern coast of California as "Ballena." Could one suppose that today's California just might have been named Ballena if colonization had begun soon after Cabrillo's exploration of 1542?

A California map of today discloses three Whale Rocks, one Whaler's Rock, and two Whaler Islands, a Whaleboat Rock, a Whalers Knoll, and a Whaleman Harbor. (J.D., W.D., B.)

Historical note: William E. Smythe reported the local whaling enterprise in his *History of San Diego:*

7

As late as the early forties [1840s], San Diego Bay was a favorite resort for female whales in their calving season, and at such times, on any bright day, scores of them could be seen basking and spouting in the sunlight. (p. 110)

The trying-works were at Ballast Point. The captured whales were towed in and cut up and the flesh thrown into two large iron pots, having a capacity of 150 gallons each. At each pot was stationed a man with a strainer, whose business it was to fish out the pieces of blubber as fast as they became sufficiently browned. These pieces were then pressed to extract the oil, after which the refuse was used for fuel. It seems to have burned very well, but made a 'villainous stench'. The oil was ladled into casks and when cool was stored awaiting shipment. (p. 111)

BANKHEAD: Settlement, Springs. Named for U.S. Senator John Hollis Bankhead of Alabama (father of actress Tallulah Bankhead). In 1916 the road through here was named Bankhead Highway to honor the senator's attempt to promote in the Congress a coast-to-coast highway which he nicknamed "The Broadway of America." Bert Horr, son of the first settler, chose this present place-name.

An early Southern California auto map indicates that Highway 80 passed through this community. However, the present Freeway 8 now loops away from Bankhead Springs just a few miles to the north. Manifestly, progress and local history did march forth — and north: the senator's name was memorialized, but "The Broadway of America," ironically, marched away from its proper place as a "pedestal" for this memorial.

For years this site has been a resort, camping, and Indian-relic-area attraction. Old Indian caves suggest their prehistoric use, since there are several springs nearby. (J.D., B.)

BANNER: Grade, Settlement, Canyon, Creek. In 1869 Louis Redman went out one day to find wild grapes — and found gold! He marked his stake with a small American flag, hence the designation of "Banner." At one time the village had a population of 1,000, 3 stores, 1 hotel, and 4 saloons. (Ha., B.)

In the 1870s Banner Grade was considered one of the most dangerous roads in the county. Today's residents there will probably warn you it still is dangerous if you drive it at a speed beyond 25 miles per hour.

BARBER MOUNTAIN. This personal name is believed to derive from George W. Barber, an early pioneer and gold miner. (J.D.) (Located northwest from Barrett Junction.)

BARKER VALLEY. This apparent personal designation in Palomar was for an early homesteader. (J.D., B.)

BARONA: Settlement, Valley, Indian Reservation, Mesa. In 1846 Senor Juan Bautista Lopez received a Mexican land grant which he titled "Cañada de San Vicente y Mesa del Padre Barona." This rather lengthy title of honor was for Padre Barona, a highly esteemed priest who ministered at San Diego Mission, 1798 - 1810. In 1933 the U.S. government purchased the Barona section of this original land grant in order to provide a reservation for the Indians who were displaced when El Capitan Dam and Reservoir were built. It is north from Alpine.

Early "project" note: In the 1880s Thomas J. Daley, a San Diego attorney, purchased a townsite in this district, having in mind to promote a model community. He built a school and church; sold small sections at low cost; and offered cattle, trees and tools at reasonable prices. The community also featured an ostrich farm. (P. Rush, pp. 99-100)

BARREL SPRING. It was a frequent pioneer practice to insert a barrel in a small spring to easily control the flow. Hence this descriptive place-name, located east from Ranchita.

BARRETT: Settlement, Junction, Dam, Reservoir, Lake. In 1919 the city of San Diego honored the Barrett family through this name designation. Pioneers in this region in the 1870s, the Barretts were extensive bee-keepers, a major industry in this part of the county before 1900. Their settlement site was earlier known as "Eisenach," so designated after a German village where Johann Sebastian Bach and Martin Luther once lived. (Ha., B.)

BATEQUITOS LAGOON. Scholars are not in agreement as to the explanation of this Spanish designation: John Davidson explained it as "the baptized ones"; Phil Hanna recorded it as "flat-bottomed boats"; and Erwin Gudde explained it as "small watering hole." (J.D., W.D., Ha., G.) (Located north from Leucadia.)

BEAR: Canyon, Creek, Ridge, Spring, Valley. This descriptive and folk place-name has been designated for at least 500 geographical features and settlements in California. The abundance of bears, especially grizzlies, all over California was unique to this state. On the map of California are 7 Bear Rivers, 25 Bear Mountains, 31 Bear Canyons, 30 Bear Valleys, over 100 Bear Creeks, etc. Further: many Bear folk-names derive from some pioneer's encounter with this formidable beast, such namings being often a remembrance of personal triumph or of desperate tragedy.

Therefore, the five Bear name-places in San Diego County can be considered to be a typical California recording of the presence of many bears years ago. *The San Diego Union,* October 31, 1879, routinely reported:

The Galsh boys of Monserrate got another big grizzly bear last week at their place called Agua Tepia (Tibia). Kytan did the shooting. He killed a large grizzly bear in the same location last year.

This name artifact highlights a special bestial threat early pioneers faced and feared in this county. (J.D., G.) It was common for sailors and travelers to report back home, "California has more bears than pigs."

BEELER CANYON. Bill Otis has resided in the Poway region for over 60 years. He reports this place-name is for Julius Buehler (sic), a German immigrant, who homesteaded 500 acres before 1900. Otis knew Julius to be a prosperous bee-keeper who always attracted notice when he drove to town in an undersized wagon drawn by two small horses and a burro.

BELL: Bluff, Valley. This apparent personal designation between Alpine and Descanso remains unexplained.

BENSON'S DRY LAKE. A personal place-name lake, located near Ocotillo Wells, and named for an early desert homesteader and prospector.

BERNARDO MOUNTAIN. Named after the Mexican land grant of 1842. (See under RANCHO BERNARDO.)

BIG HORN CANYON. An obvious descriptive designation in Anza-Borrego Desert for the presence of wild sheep.

BIG LAGUNA. (See under LAGUNA.)

BIG WASH. A descriptive designation in northeast Anza-Borrego Desert.

Early trappers brought "wash" into the American language, applying it to designate the dry bed of a stream. Since this desert receives only 4 - 5 inches rainfall annually, climate and season create innumerable "washes." (G. Stewart, p. 220)

BIRCH HILL. When "greenhorn" British brothers, Arthur and Harry Birch, chose to settle on Palomar Mountain, they built a cabin — with great perseverance yet little experience — and with no doors or windows! They entered and exited their home through an opening under the roof by means of a ladder. After a period of pioneering, they sold out and returned to England. Arthur died in the Boer War. When Harry became Lord Birch by inheritance, local settlers must have been honored and thrilled by the fact that "Lord Harry" had once lived among them as "Greenhorn" Harry. (C. Wood, p. 67)

BISNAGA ALTA WASH. A descriptive place-name that translates from the Spanish as "tall barrel cactus." It is located in Anza-Borrego Desert.

Such a plant is able to store up moisture in its interior spongelike mass. The leathery exterior prevents evaporation. Experienced desert dwellers and travelers used the barrel cactus as a water source in emergencies. Its bland, yet drinkable water had been known and used for years by Mexicans who lived in arid locales. (J.S. Chase, p. 368)

BITTER CREEK: Canyon, Spring. A descriptive name for the palatability of water, always of concern to early trappers, cattlemen, prospectors and surveyors. Hence its designation. (Southeast from Ranchita.)

A "creek" in Britain signified a river that was an arm of the sea, and early Eastern colonists accordingly applied it similarly. Growth of American language changed "creek" to "river," applying the former as the meaning for a small stream. (G. Stewart, p. 60)

BLACK: Mountains, Canyon. There have been 3 Black Mountains in the county. One of these, in Mission Valley, flaunts the prominent "S," a symbol for the nearby state university; it was earlier known as Mission Peak to indicate its prominent location in Mission Valley. Later it was named Cowles Mountain after an early El Cajon rancher. (See also under COWLES MOUNTAIN.)

Black Mountain in the Peñasquitos district, according to *The San Diego Herald,* was reported to have been the location of the first gold mine in California in 1828.

A third Black Mountain is in Santa Ysabel Valley, an area of unusual scenic attraction. (J.D., B.) (See also under MOUNT GOWER.)

As a descriptive place-name, "Black" is a common mountain designation throughout California and the U.S., either due to dark geological composition, or to the atmospheric effect on growth on mountain slopes.

BLAIR VALLEY. According to *The San Diego Union,* November 13, 1893, Blair Valley was probably named "for a settler in the Julian country, known as Samuel Blair or 'Bronco Sam.' "

BLOW SAND CANYON. Such a concise, folk-type place-name describes a location of a windy canyon. Today's sportlife motorcyclists and dune buggyists throng here on weekends to challenge the steep, slithering obstacle of a large sand dune in this canyon. (Ocotillo Wells.)

BODEN CANYON. Named for an early homesteader in the Santa Ysabel area who migrated to California from Germany (according to Jeff Swycoffer, Postmaster at Santa Ysabel).

BONEYARD CANYON. This descriptive name at Barrett Lake remains unexplained. Was an Indian cemetery discovered here? Was it a place of strewn cattle bones? Were suspect prehistoric bones found here when Barrett Dam was being constructed?

"Boneyard" is a typical example of a folk-name.

BONITA. (Spanish for "pretty" or "good.") This descriptively named settlement is a parcel of the El Rancho Nacional Mexican land grant of 1845. In 1884 settler Henry F. Cooper owned the "Bonita Ranch." A fruit-packing center developed here in 1891, retaining the designation of "Bonita." Song composer H.H. Higgins pioneered in this area in 1893, seeking a place to improve his health. His "Hang Up The Baby's Stockings" and "Nobody Cares But Me" were very popular songs near the close of the nineteenth century. (J.D.)

Earlier county population (U.S. Census Bureau):	
1850 – 798 persons	1890 – 34,987 persons
1860 – 1,324 persons	1900 – 35,090 persons
1870 – 4,951 persons	1910 – 61,665 persons
1880 – 8,618 persons	
(Indians not included in the above.)	

BONSALL. Originally named "Mt. Fairview," this settlement was later changed to "Osgood" after the chief engineer who was in charge of the Southern Railroad Survey in this area in the 1870s. Locals applied "Osgood" with the hope of influencing the railroad to run its tracks through or adjacent to their settlement – all to no avail. Finally, a petition for a post office in 1889 recommended the names of "Reed," "Favorite," or "Bonsall." Post Office headquarters in Washington, D.C., chose "Bonsall," the name of a retired Methodist minister who developed a fruit-tree nursery here in 1889, and of whom

The San Diego Union and Daily Bee reported September 7, 1889:

> Mr. James Bonsall purchased his property of a settler in 1879 and immediately moved on to commence active operations with a cash capital of $3.00. His enterprise was successful.

BORREGO: Badlands, Mountain, Palm Canyon, Springs, Desert, Valley, Wells, Sink, Sink Wash. ("Borrego" means "lamb" in Spanish.) Borrego Springs was considered to have been an important watering place for the abundant big-horn sheep in the valley and in the mountains. This place-name, often applied by the Spanish throughout California, derives its designation from these wild sheep. Manifestly, it was a favorite hunting ground for Indians, Mexicans, and Yankees.

It is believed that Anza and his desert party camped at the southern end of Borrego Valley to provide rest for their animals. Indian shards offered evidence that a large Indian settlement once existed here. A lingering legend has it that Borrego Springs in the early 1870s was the abode of Negro Jim Green, one of the first gold prospectors in the district. (J.D., W.D.)

Borrego Badlands are a spectacular mud formation that attracts many desert tourists.

Language note: When a district had many ravines that were difficult to travel through, French fur trappers applied "mauvaise terre" to such a site. American fur trappers borrowed the phrase to make it the concise yet foreboding Yankee phrase, "badlands." (G. Stewart, p. 220) (See also under FONTS POINT.)

BOSTONIA. This transferred or borrowed name derives from a group of Bostonians who settled here in 1887 to cultivate citrus fruits and raisin grapes on their Boston ranch. Raisins from this area took first prize at the Paris Exposition of 1889. (J.D., W.D., B.)

Historical agricultural memo: *The San Diego County Advertiser,* September 10, 1891, reported:

El Cajon raisin pickers pronounce this year's crop the finest in quality ever produced in the valley...In 1890 the crop was about 85 carloads, or 127,500 boxes. This year (1891) it will be from 125 to 150 carloads, or 187,500 boxes to 225,000 boxes. The latter figure being considered a fair one, El Cajon has 4,500,000 pounds of raisins to sell at the present figure of four cents a pound.

BOTTLE: Peak, Spring. A descriptive form of place-name for the shape of this peak. (South from Lake Wohlford.)

BOUCHER HILL. An apparent misspelling for "Bougher," a pioneer family in Palomar district. A Forest Service lookout station now stands at this point. (J.D., B.)

BOULDER: Creek, Oaks. A tributary of the San Diego River, Boulder Creek is considered to be a most picturesque stream of water rushing amid boulders and rocks southwest from Julian. Boulder Oaks is an attractive locale on the Campo Road near La Posta, and it is most aptly described by its place-name. (J.D., W.D., B.)

Ten gold mine claims once existed near this creek, according to researcher Winifred Davidson.

BOULEVARD. A type of descriptive name for a small trading settlement near Jacumba. Its settlers designated the highway through their center as a "boulevard" leading into Imperial Valley. (G.)

BOUNDARY: Peak, Spring. Surveyors frequently designated this name for a geographical feature which served as a checking point for a survey in the area. Boundary Peak is located immediately north of the Mexican border about 10 miles southwest from Jacumba. (G.)

BOW WILLOW: Canyon, Peak, Creek. This descriptive designation is located southeast from Agua Caliente Springs State Park in Anza-Borrego Desert. The desert willow is a small tree with narrow leaves and fragrant flowers, frequently extending 20 feet high, and usually growing best in desert washes. (J.S. Chase, p. 369)

The canyon is a popular camping site for desert weekenders.

BOX CANYON. This descriptive location for a narrow and rocky passage through hills near San Felipe Valley is now a state historical monument. It was a famous pass on what became known as the Southern Emigrant Trail. The route from Arizona went west through Carrizo Wash, Vallecitos, and Warner Springs. General Kearney and Kit Carson passed this way to the battle of San Pasqual. In 1847 the Mormon Battalion cut a passage through this canyon which enabled the first pioneer wagons to proceed into southwest California, thereby establishing the Southern Emigrant Trail. Gold field emigrants struggled through it in 1849. Butterfield Overland Mail Stages used it in 1858-61. It soon became a district for desert travelers, gold-seekers, Mexican immigrants, Civil War deserters, and desperados. After the close of the Civil War the quartering of U.S. soldiers at Vallecitos State Station brought some law and order to this outpost and to the route of travel. The first mule-pack mail train (the "Jackass Mail") used this canyon as a route from Yuma to San Diego. (J.D., W.D.)

Another Box Canyon is situated in Collins Valley near the Riverside County line.

BRATTON VALLEY. Napoleon Bratton was an early settler and cattleman in this valley north from Dulzura. He started with Spanish longhorns and later bred them with Durhams, thereby improving his herd. (J.D., B.)

17

> Historical note: In his *History of San Diego,* William E. Smythe recorded that agriculture never reached an important stage during Spanish and Mexican domination. Instead, cattle-raising was the chief industry:
>
> The easy-going inhabitants were well content if they produced enough to meet their own needs, and their methods and implements were ridiculously crude. Until the Americans came there were no plows in the country except those made of the fork of a tree shod with a flat piece of iron. Grain was cut with a short sickle, and horses threshed it with their hooves.
>
> But while the agricultural experience was a hard struggle from the beginning, the livestock industry was rapidly developed without encountering any difficulties. It involved but little labor. . .for it could be done mostly on horseback with long intervals of rest between the periods of activity. The pasturage was usually excellent, and the cattle took care of themselves and multiplied prodigiously. The Mission Fathers were, of course, the fathers of the cattle business. It was not until the commodity acquired a population apart from that sheltered by the Presidio and the Mission that private herds began to appear, but the success of the Fathers inevitably attracted others into the profitable business of raising cattle on free pastures. (p. 100)

BUBBLING SPRINGS. An apt and descriptive name-designation, located in Tubb Canyon within Anza-Borrego Desert. (See also under TUBB CANYON.)

BUCKSNORT MOUNTAIN. Origin of place-name unknown. Located north from Warner Springs, this might be a form of folk-name relating to an incident here with deer.

BUENA: Settlement, Creek. (Spanish for "good.") This descriptive place-name was a parcel from the Buena Vista Rancho, a Mexican land grant awarded to Indian neophyte Felipe Subria, one of the few Indians to be that lucky. The rancho was purchased by Cave J. Couts some years later. In 1890 the San Diego Central Railroad crossed this rancho, establishing the station of Buena Vista. In 1908 a nearby station name was shortened to "Buena."

Rancho historian R.W. Brackett *(History of San Diego County Ranchos)* perhaps explained the good luck in 1844 of the Indian Felipe Subria:

> At this time the acquisition of land was almost ridiculously simple for those in political favor. The prospective rancher paid perhaps $12 for papers, swore that he was a Mexican citizen and a Catholic, and stated the number of square leagues he desired. On one occasion a petitioner applied for a moderate amount of land and was told that it was too small for consideration — he was obliged to accept several times as much or get nothing.

> The ranchero usually named his holdings for the patron saint of his family or the saint upon whose holy day the grant was made. Sometimes he adopted the Indian name, as in the case of Guajome (Indian for "home of the frogs") Rancho. Occasionally, the name was descriptive of regional characteristics, as in Buena Vista (Spanish for "good view")....One Californian, evidently in doubt as to which saints were most deserving of the honor, named his holdings the Rancho Santa Ana y Quien Sabe (Spanish for "Saint Ann and Who Knows?"). (pp. 12-13)

BUENA VISTA: Lagoon, Creek. (Spanish for "attractive view.") This is a name designation after the Buena Vista Rancho. The lagoon flows into the Pacific Ocean south of Carlsbad. *The San Diego Union,* October 8, 1938, reported that a drive was on to make this estuary an official bird sanctuary, for it long had been a refuge for several species of wildfowl. Buena Vista Creek empties into the lagoon. Another Buena Vista Creek is located east of Lake Henshaw. Its name antedates that of Buena Vista Rancho and it has no connection with this ranch. The creek was first mentioned in 1821 by a group of padres and soldiers exploring in the northern section of the county. (J.D., W.D.)

Historical note: When San Luis Rey Mission was founded in 1798, its grazing lands included much of northern San Diego County and southern Riverside County. The ending of Mexican occupation in California brought disposal of these extensive Mission holdings. Buena Vista Rancho had been a section of this former property of San Luis Rey Mission. (P. Rush, p. 16)

BURNT MOUNTAIN. Name designation remains unexplained. Was it so named because of a spectacular fire on its slopes? Was an Indian village wiped out here by fire? Was a pioneer's home destroyed here by fire? (North from Escondido.)

BURRO SPRINGS. Was this a place where wild burros came to drink? (Located near Agua Caliente Springs.)

BUTLER CANYON. The source of this personal designation is a part of desert folk-history: the canyon was named as a mocking or sneering reminder of a mining prospector who was discovered to be a fraud. He failed to find gold in this canyon where he had guaranteed it would be. Thereafter, it was common to refer to any desert fraud — or failure — as "a Butler." (L. Reed, pp. 65-66) (Located north from Borrego Springs.)

BUTTES: Canyon, Pass. This descriptive designation located in Anza-Borrego Desert probably refers to its geographical small "butte" feature.

American fur trappers borrowed "butte" from the French fur men who used it to describe a sharp hill rising from a plain. (G. Stewart, p. 220)

BUTTEWEG CREEK. An unexplained place-name located in the San Ysidro Mountains at the Mexican border.

BY JIM SPRING. An apparent folk-name for a natural feature in Tubb Canyon. (See also under TUBB CANYON.)

CABRILLO NATIONAL MONUMENT. Located on the headlands of Point Loma, overlooking the Pacific and the Port of San Diego, this aesthetic memorial was established in 1913. It is known as the place where the West and California began, with the arrival here of Captain Juan Rodriguez Cabrillo in 1542. Vizcaino in 1602 constructed a simple prayer shelter atop this headland.

A lighthouse, a visitors' center of fine historic exhibits, and an imposing statue of Cabrillo, in a garden setting, enhance the magnificent panorama of ocean, harbor, and landscape. (See also under SAN DIEGO.)

CALAVERA: Peak, Lake. (Spanish for "skull.") These identical place-names are for a low elevation and a small adjacent lake located east from Carlsbad. The origin of this twin naming is not known.

Such a Spanish folk-name was occasionally applied throughout California, referring to bones found that suggested Indian remains, personal pioneer tragedy, or even famine. One of California's 58 counties is named "Calaveras" to designate the large number of skulls and skeletons found extensively in that county about 1838. (G.)

CAMERON: Corners, Station, Valley. *The San Diego Union,* October 27, 1870, reported this station as part of the Yuma-San Diego stagecoach route. Thomas Cameron, pioneer stockman, was the first settler in this valley (north from Campo). The Indian place-name was believed to have been "Musquat," signifying a "place of red dirt." (J.D.)

CAMP PENDLETON. The enthusiastic leadership of Major General Joseph Pendleton resulted in the establishment of this famous Marine base. A popular military officer who was affectionately nicknamed "Uncle Joe" by rank-and-file soldiers, Pendleton served in the Marine Corps for 40 years.

Name-game-wane: Originally addressed as "Camp J.H. Pendleton, Santa Margarita Ranch, California," it soon became "Camp Pendleton, Oceanside, California," later changing to "Camp Pendleton, San Diego, California," and finally shrinking to "Camp Pendleton, California." (Robt. M. Witty and Neil Morgan, *Marines of the Margarita,* p. 69.) (See also under JOFEGAN and SANTA MARGARITA.)

CAMPO: Settlement, Station, Valley, Lake, Indian Reservation. (Spanish for "field.") Finding an extensive Indian village there, it probably was pertinent for the early Spanish and Mexicans to designate this as a "campo." The Mexican border was an active district for cattle rustlers and desperados who were fleeing from justice on either side of the border. Army deserters and Civil War refugees from Texas often halted at Campo to try their luck – and experiment with opportunity – at cattle raising or farming or anything. As a matter of record, this area around Campo became nicknamed "New Texas" due to its numerous Lone Star immigrants and opportunists.

"Wild West" tale note: In 1869 the Gaskill brothers opened a trading store here. A dramatic robbery attempt of their store by Mexican desperados was reported in *The San Diego Union* of December 5, 1895, and this newspaper account has all the excitement of a Hollywood "shoot 'em up" script.

The Indian name for this district was "Milquataj" for either "big foot" or "wide valley." (J.D., Hu., W.D.)

CAÑADA VERRUGA. (Spanish for "wart valley.") Local tradition reports that an Indian squatter homesteaded south from Warner Springs in 1864. He was highly regarded for his superior intelligence. Due to a large wart on his neck he was nicknamed "Verruga" by the Mexicans in the area. Thereby the nickname was applied to his ranch and to the valley of his abode. (Hu.)

CANEBRAKE: Wash, Canyon. A descriptive designation south of Agua Caliente Springs after the wild canebrakes found here. (Hu.)

CANYON CITY. An apt descriptive place-name for a small rustic settlement tucked away in a canyon pocket southwest from Campo. It is an attractive recreational location. A store with bar has been operated here for years under the name of "Dogpatch Cafe," and its owner has sought to have the settlement renamed "Dogpatch." A local trailer camp owner reported that the settlement residents rejected such a name.

CAPITAN GRANDE RESERVATION. (Spanish for "Big Captain.") The Indian name for this village was "Quil-ach-nusk" or "long valley." The reservation, north from Alpine, was set by executive order of President Grant on December 27, 1875. (J.D.)

In 1931 the most desirable part of this preserve was purchased by the City of San Diego for construction of a dam. The purchase gave the Capitan Grande and Los Conejos tribes money to buy land in the Barona Reservation area.

Helen Hunt Jackson visited Capitan Grande in 1883. In *Century of Dishonor,* she wrote:

These Indians have continued ever since to live there, although latterly they have been so much pressed upon by the white settlers that their numbers have been reduced. A large reservation, showing on the record nineteen full sections, was set off here in 1876 (sic) for these Indians. As usual, their village site was not taken in by the lines. Therefore white settlers have come in and the Indians have been driven away. . . .There are now about sixty Indians left in this canyon. Sixteen years ago there were from one hundred and fifty to two hundred — a flourishing community with large herds of cattle and horses and good cultivated fields. It is not too late for the Government to reclaim the greater part of this canyon for its rightful owners' use. (p. 497)

CARDIFF BY THE SEA. This is a form of transferred or borrowed name from the seaport in Wales, and it was so designated by Frank Cullen, developer of this site. Its earlier place-name was "San Elijo" after the nearby lagoon of the same name. The area had been a popular beach and fishing site for a long time. The town originally was part of Los Encinitos Rancho. Developer Cullen nostalgically applied British place-names to all his streets, most of which remain today. High-grade clay deposits which were commercially shipped out of the state existed here for a long time. (J.D., G.)

CARL SPRING. An apparent personal place-name whose identity remains unknown. (Descanso district.)

CARLSBAD: Settlement, State Beach. (German for "Charles's watering place:") Pioneer John Frazier home-steaded here in 1883, and soon it was known as Frazier's Station. Digging for a well in 1886, he discovered mineral water. Analysis declared this water to be equal in mineral content to that of Karlsbad, Bohemia. Hence the place-name (with a *C!*). During World War I high patriotism shrank this name to "Carl," the original name being restored once the war hysteria ended. (Ha., W.D.)

Early boom town memo: In the 1890s an anonymous local resident (full of poetic enthusiasm and rockinghorse rhythm) superlatively rhapsodized:

There's a fountain in the mountain
O'er the summit by the shore,
Where the sea-winds and the lea-winds
Meet and mingle ever more.

It is Carlsbad, bonny Carlsbad
And upon its sparkling brink
Hygeia sits forever smiling —
And she bids you come and drink.

Are you ailing, are you failing,
Have you ilk you cannot tell?
There is healing past revealing
In the waters of the well.

It is Carlsbad, bonny Carlsbad
And upon its sparkling brink
Hygeia sits forever smiling —
And she bids you come and drink.

CARMEL: Mountain, Valley. (Hebrew for the Biblical *Karmel,* "vineyard or fruitful field.") This is a type of transferred place-name for a site east of Torrey Pines State Reserve.

CARNEY CANYON. This personal place-name was for William Carney who came to the Santa Maria Rancho district as a stockman.

CARRIZO: Badlands, Canyon, Creek, Gorge, Mountain, Palms, Valley. (Spanish for "reed grass" or "cane.") This descriptive place-name repeatedly was applied throughout early California because of the function of the carrizo for the Indians as a sweetening substance ("panoche" to the Indians). It was mentioned in 1775 by Padre Font when the Anza exploration camped south of Agua Caliente Hot Springs.

The plant is a reed grass or cane with long, narrow

leaves that can be up to 10 feet in length. It is usually found in damp places in open desert. (J.S. Chase, p. 376)

These "badlands" in southern Anza-Borrego Desert are a barren, rugged, and forbidding (yet spectacular) feature of the mountains on each side of the creek. The valley temperature is often extremely hot.

Carrizo was a station for the "Jackass" mail train from Yuma to San Diego. (J.D., W.D.)

CARROLL CANYON. This personal designation was for Thomas Carroll, a pioneer settler. *The San Diego Union,* September 20, 1891, reported:

> Thomas Carroll's five-acre orchard, planted six years ago in the valley, is loaded this season with apricots, pears, peaches, figs and lemons.

Carroll's ranch was located north of Miramar Naval Air Station. (J.D.)

Back county boom memo (from County Assessment lists of 1891):	
Number of fruit trees under cultivation	
1887	91,148
1888	191,526
1889	380,176
1890	511,742
1891	1,062,711
San Diego County Advertiser, July 25, 1891	

CASE SPRING. Place-named for Alden B. Case who settled in San Luis Rey district in 1894 as a farmer.

CASTRO CANYON. A personal place-name, located near Pala, for either Ramon or Zacarias Castro who lived in this canyon.

CEDAR: Canyon, Creek. A descriptive designation for the evergreens that grew here west from Dulzura.

"Cedar" was a landmark of nature for the trappers and early pioneers, for it usually indicated the presence of a water source. (G. Stewart, p. 222)

CHAPPO. Designation of this Spanish name remains unknown. The site was a cattle-loading station on the Santa Margarita Ranch. (J.D.)

Historical Cattle Note: In *History of San Diego*, William E. Smythe wrote:

The range steer was the first historical character in the commercial life of San Diego. It was he who drew the ships from far-off New England; furnished material for an export trade with the United States, Mexico, South America, and the Sandwich Islands; and even laid the foundations of social life at Old Town by supplying an interest to attract and support a population, including some families of large means, when the military society began to pass away. Every early visitor to San Diego refers to the hide-houses which stood out conspicuously near La Playa (Pt. Loma) and which, for many years, served as the emblem of its commercial importance. (p. 98)

CHARIOT: Canyon, Mountain. The famous Golden Chariot gold mine was discovered and named in 1871 by George King in a canyon south from Banner. It was considered to be the richest gold strike in southern California. In a span of three years, and less than 200 feet below the surface, almost $1,000,000 in gold was found here. (J.D.)

CHERRY CANYON. Did a cherry orchard once exist here in Ranchita district? Or were there wild berry shrubs that appeared cherry-like?

CHICARITA CREEK. Probably a Yankee mispronunciation of *chiquita* (Spanish for "very little"), an apt description for this small creek in Peñasquitas district. (J.D.)

CHIHUAHUA: Creek, Valley. Goatherder Jose Melandras

homesteaded near Warner Springs in an isolated location. The influx of immigrants into the district forced him to seek renewed solitude farther away in a valley that he named after the Mexican state of his origin. (G.)

CHILKOOT PASS. An old-time Dulzura settler reported this place-name for the first wagon road through Bratton Valley as a transferred name of the same pass of Klondike fame, stating that its twin designation remained a mystery.

CHIMNEY: Creek, Lake, Rock, Spring. Rock formations often suggested a name designation or signpost for early trappers and pioneers. Gudde reports over 30 Chimney place-names throughout California. The famous Chimney Rock of Nebraska was a natural signpost for early wagon trains westward. It is now known as Chimney Rock National Historic Site. San Diego Chimney sites are quite small and insignificant by comparison.

CHRISTIANITOS CANYON. (Originally was *Cristianitos.*) Two priests with the Portola expedition in 1769 christened two dying Indian infants in this canyon north from San Onofre.

Historical note: Padre Crespi named 170 places on the Portola expedition of 1769 as it traveled north to find Monterey. Only 30 of these original place-names are on today's map of California, and four of these are still in San Diego County: Christianitos Canyon, Santa Margarita River, San Elijo Lagoon, and Encinitas. (G.)

CHUCKAWALLA: Wash, Canyon. A descriptive designation located in Anza-Borrego Desert, named for a species of lizard of the southwest.

CHULA VISTA: City, Reservoir. (Spanish for "pretty or magnificent view.") This was a boom town in 1887 which quickly became a prominent citrus-growing center. Later it was reported that "the largest lemon orchard in the world" existed here. Years later the celery harvest was an important crop in the community. (J.D., W.D.)

In 1974 the population of Chula Vista was the second largest in the county.

CIENEGA FLATS. (Spanish for "marshy place.") This descriptive form of name west from Lake Henshaw combines a Spanish adjective with an American noun, perhaps to retain a Spanish atmosphere. This hybrid form of place-naming occurred frequently throughout California.

CLARK: Dry Lake, Valley, Well. Fred and Frank Clark were prominent cattlemen of Coyote Canyon region. According to author Lester Reed, a contemporary of the Clarks, in *Old Time Cattlemen and Other Pioneers of Anza-Borrego,* when Frank and Fred Clark began their search on the desert for possible cattle-range where water could be developed, they traveled on foot, taking along a burro to carry water, food, and a light bedroll. (pp. 35-36)

During World War II the dry lake was used for aerial practice. Thus this site's geographical and historical dwellers included the early Indians, the later cattle grazers, and finally the modern military.

The first permanent Borrego Desert well to be dug in the twentieth century probably was the Clark Well (1906), the work of pioneer cattlemen Frank and Fred Clark. In "Patrol Notes, Borrego State Park, 1955" Park Ranger Jack Welch reported that the Clark brothers started their well-digging at 10:00 A.M. one day. By 11:00 P.M. they watered their horses from a well fifteen feet deep. However, by 1948 the Clark Well had dried out.

CLEVELAND NATIONAL FOREST. Officially named and proclaimed in 1909 to honor President Cleveland who had a special interest in federal forestry promotion. This preserve is one of the oldest in the U.S., having been set aside in 1893. The object of this preservation was to protect its watershed areas. It contained the headwaters of the San Diego, Sweetwater, and San Luis Rey rivers and their tributaries. The Cuyamaca Mountains are among its highest peaks. (J.D., W.D.)

CLEVENGER CANYON. A personal place-name in the Ramona district for early settler Archibald Clevenger who came to California in 1849 from Tennessee. (J.D.)

CLOVER FLAT. This descriptive name-designation can be found in many places throughout the U.S. (Northeast from Campo.)

COLB VALLEY. Named for homesteader William Kolb (sic) of Palomar district, remembered as a giant of a man of unusual strength. (J.D.)

COLD SPRING. A descriptive place-name for a spring in Cuyamaca region reported to have the coldest water in San Diego County. Its Indian name was "Oh-ha-wee-ah-ha," signifying "water colder water." (J.D.)

The generic terms (cold, coldwater) in Spanish and English appear in more than 100 places in California. (G.)

COLEMAN: Creek, Flat. This personal name designated Fred Coleman, a Negro settler. He and Elza Wood discovered gold in this creek (south from Santa Ysabel). The ore was not of first-grade quality. (J.D.)

COLLINS VALLEY. Place-named for squatter Collins who jumped the claim of an earlier homesteader. A government survey team in 1901 designated this place-name (north from Borrego Springs).

COMBS PEAK. The derivation of this apparent personal place-name is not known. It is one of the highest peaks in San Diego County (north from Warner Springs).

French trappers said "pic" for the points of mountains. Yankee fur men Americanized it as "peak." (G. Stewart, p. 221)

CONEJOS: Creek, Valley. (Spanish for "rabbits.") The Indian name for this creek was reported as "Halsch-yoh-na-wah," signifying "place of the cottontail rabbit." Apparently the early Spanish in this district tagged the nickname of "Conejos" to the Indian tribe that lived along this creek (west from Cuyamaca Peak). (J.D.)

COOPER: Canyon, Cienega. A personal form of place-name whose identity remains unexplained; it is located northeast from Oak Grove.

CORONADO. (Spanish for "crown.") In 1602 Vizcaino sighted and named the offshore Coronado Islands after the four Coronado brothers who were martyred in early Rome by Emperor Diocletian. Local history reports that the town of Coronado was named after these offshore islands. In 1886 Elisha Babcock (a railroad financier) and H.L. Story (Story Piano Company) organized Coronado Beach Company. They planned to build a resort hotel with a town around it. The resulting Coronado Hotel is world-famous. (D.)

The following sidelight by H.G. Otis in the *Los Angeles Times*, May 13, 1886, reported:

> . . .in every deed a stipulation is inserted that no spiritous liquors shall ever be sold or drunk on the premises. People who want to get drunk must do so at the hotel which reserves a monopoly on the beer business. The prohibition, I learn, is causing a good many kicks but the owners stand

firm, maintaining it would be the ruin of the spot to allow it to be covered with saloons. . . .They have planted themselves solid on the rock of prohibition — with a loophole in the hotel to get into. They believe in temperance, but they are not bigoted about it.

Other enterprises soon included restaurants, a bowling alley, a Japanese Tea House, and an ostrich farm.

Historical entrepreneur memo: A classified ad in *The San Diego County Advertiser,* August 20, 1891, announced:

OSTRICHES — a rare opportunity to get a glimpse of AFRICA — don't fail to visit the Ostrich Farms either at Coronado or at Fallbrook. A beautiful assortment of dressed Plumes and Tips for sale. E.J. Johnson, Fallbrook, or 10th and B, Coronado.

Coronado and North Island are located on what once was a grant of over 4,000 acres named "Peninsula de San Diego Rancho." Pedro C. Carillo received the grant in 1846 from Governor Pio Pico, the site being described as "land big enough for 2 grazing sites." (R.W. Brackett, p. 48 ff.)

It is believed that Vizcaino in 1602 dug wells on North Island to supply his crew with fresh water. (P. Rush, p. 50 ff.) (See also under NORTH ISLAND and PENIN-SULA DE SAN DIEGO RANCHO.)

CORRAL CANYON: Mountain, Spring. This descriptive place-name designated the open space on a peak in Mesa Grande which resembled a corral encircled by brush and trees. Corral Canyon Spring in Morena Valley also may be named for an animal corral that existed there at one time. (J.D.)

CORTE MADERA: Lake, Mountain, Valley. (Spanish for "woodyard," a place where timbers were felled.) It is reported that this Spanish place-name in Pine Valley district dates back to the building of missions in the county.

James E. Flinn (for whom Flinn Springs is named) fearlessly pioneered in this district near Pine Valley in 1874 even though he was warned that he faced hostility from the Indians in the area. Years later Spreckels and others owned a large parcel in this area which they maintained as a private game preserve. (J.D.) (See also under FLINN SPRINGS.)

COSMIT: Peak, Indian Reservation. Reported to be an early Indian name whose meaning is unknown. In 1875 an official order by President Grant set this area aside as an Indian reservation.

The site is about 20 miles south from Julian and just east of Inaja Indian Reservation. Cosmit Preserve comprises 80 acres, and it was once used by Inaja natives for grazing purposes only. As of 1972 no Indians were reported living on Cosmit Reservation. (L. Swain, p. 129)

COTTONWOOD: Creek, Canyon, Valley. Five Cottonwood Creeks were designated in San Diego County. *The San Diego Union,* January 5, 1887, reported that Yankees in a district applied "Cottonwood Creek" to the same stream that Mexican settlers had named "Jesus Maria Creek."

When early trappers and pioneers saw a dark, green line across the desert, they hoped cottonwoods were there in the distance, indicating that such trees stood at a stream, or that water could be had by digging in the sand beneath these trees. Often such a site contained pasturage for horses and cattle. (G. Stewart, p. 222)

COUGAR CANYON. Mispronunciation ranged an odd gamut at this Borrego Park locale: according to Park Ranger Jack Welch, this gorge was named "Krueger" Canyon to honor George Krueger, Secretary of the

Brawley Chamber of Commerce. In just a few years the honorable gentleman was probably surprised and understandably quite dismayed to learn that local usage had transformed him into a "Cougar"!

The canyon's Indian name of "Mul-lul" remains unexplained.

COUSER CANYON. Long-time resident Jim Yarger was born and raised in San Luis Rey district. He reported that R.V. Couser was a lumberman from northern California who purchased the Ormsby Ranch in the canyon that now bears Couser's name. Yarger recalled that Couser settled here about 1900 as a farmer.

COWLES MOUNTAIN. George A. Cowles was a prominent pioneer in El Cajon Valley who experimented with the cultivation of grapes and olives. His raisins were shipped throughout the states.

This innovative pioneer's name has had an on-again-off-again location on county maps: "Dog Spring" on this mountain earlier was named "Cowles Spring," "Cowles Mountain" was once changed to "Black Mountain," and now reappears on maps as "Cowles Mountain," and the use of the name of "Cowles Ranch" was later changed to "Santee" in an interesting and "romantic" switch. (See under SANTEE.) (Ha.)

COYOTE: Canyon, Peak, Mountain, Valley, Creek. This Anza-Borrego descriptive "cluster" name was frequently applied throughout the Southwest.

Ecology memo: *The Los Angeles Times,* May 20, 1975, reported:

> Coyote Canyon will be closed for the first time in summer months so bighorn sheep in the Anza-Borrego Desert State Park will not be afraid to come down for water. The California Parks and Recreation Department announced that motorists will be barred from the popular canyon

roadway from July 1 to Sept. 30. The closure is expected to benefit nursing ewes and young lambs, especially of the endangered bighorn species, which is protected from hunters by state law, a spokesman said.

CRESTWOOD. This is a descriptive place-name in Campo district.

CUCA RANCHO. (See under LA JOLLA INDIAN RES-VATION and RODRIGUEZ MOUNTAIN.)

CULP: Canyon, Valley, Spring. John Kolp (sic) was an early cattleman in the Ranchita district. Borrego Park Ranger Jack Welch reported that Kolp applied this personal name to these sites adjacent to Tubb Canyon. (See also under TUBB CANYON.)

CUTCA VALLEY. Long-time resident Alice Bergman reported that this place-name was pronounced "Whitka" when she was a child. Over the years the name became mispronounced as "Cutca." Mrs. Bergman also stated the meaning and origin of "Whitka" was always a mystery to earlier residents in her childhood years. (Located north from Palomar.)

CUYAMACA: Peak, Valley, Lake, Settlement. (From the Indian *ekui-amak.*) The meaning of this name is varied: "rain from above," "rain from behind," and "place beyond the rain." Its spelling and pronunciation likewise varied: in 1827 mission padres mention it as "Sierra de Cuyamat." Later it appeared as Cuyamac, Kyamanc, Quiamac, and even as Queermack. (J.D., W.D.)

In 1845 Rancho Cuyamaca was granted to Don Augustin Olvera, the same Californio of Olvera Street prominence in Los Angeles. He sold the grant in 1869. Imagine his dismay when gold was discovered in this district one year later!

Mary Elizabeth Johnson wrote in *Indian Legends of the Cuyamacas:*

Cuyamaca probably is a Spanish corruption of the Indian *Kwe-ah-mac,* a name they (the Indians) used first to designate a location high in the middle mountain, but later applied it to the entire group. These mountains had distinctive names also. The one farthest north, they called E-yee (Nest) because they believed that a big nest or den was on one of its slopes in which the wild animals disappeared when hunted, thus safely ending pursuit. The middle one, Hal-kwo-kwilsh (Tough Strong), gained this title in the battle of the Peaks when he proved very formidable. The one known as the Cuyamaca Peak acquired the name of Poo-k-sqwee (Crooked Neck) in this same battle. And before the battle still another peak, Hilsh-ki-e (Pine Tree) belonged to the group, so the Indians say, but now lives far away. (Adapted from p. 8) (See also under GREEN VALLEY.)

CUYAPAIPA INDIAN RESERVATION. (Indian for "leaning rock" or "rock-lie-on.") This was the site of an earlier Indian tribe. Also spelled as "Weapipe" and "Guyapipe." Located in the Laguna Mountain district, it included over 4000 acres, most of which are suitable only for grazing. A small part of this reserve could be irrigated and dry farmed. In 1972 only one native resident was reported here. The reservation was established by Presidential executive order in 1875. (L. Swain, p. 132)

CYPRESS CANYON. This is a common descriptive name-form found throughout the U.S. (This site is in Miramar district.)

DALY: Creek, Mine. An apparent personal name whose identity has not been ascertained. (Located northeast from Lakeside.)

DAMERON VALLEY. Named for Mit Damron (sic) who was brought to California by covered wagon when he was two years old. He settled in Palomar district in the 1860s and became a prominent cattleman. Damron ranged most of his cattle in canyons of Anza-Borrego Desert.

DANEY CANYON. The identity of this personal place-name remains unknown. (Ramona district.)

DEADMAN: Flat, Hole. Folk-names for sites in Santa Ysabel and Warner Springs where dead bodies were discovered. (J.D.)

DEER: Canyon, Park, Lake, Spring. This is a common descriptive or folk place-name. The deer ranks second to the bear as a place-name repeated all over California. (G.)

DEERHORN: Valley, Spring. Probably so named when deerhorn was found at these Barrett Lake sites.

DEGUYNOS CANYON. Such a Spanish place-name appears to be a corruption for "Diegueños," a reference to Indians whose lands at one time were considered to be under the control and use of San Diego Mission. (In similar manner, Luiseño Indians were considered wards of San Luis Rey Mission.) The canyon is in Anza-Borrego Desert.

DEL DIOS. (Spanish for "God's Place.") Mrs. Frances Ryan, longtime resident and author-historian of the Escondido district, reported that Del Dios was a land development of this century. It eventually was annexed to Escondido.

DEL MAR. City, Mesa. (Spanish for "oceanside" or "by the sea.") Col. J.S. Taylor, land surveyor and Indian scout for Buffalo Bill, came to the settlement of Weed in 1882. He soon was promoting a land subdivision, and he built a grandiose hotel. Part of the real estate promotion was the selection of a more romantic village name. "Del Mar" was suggested by Mrs. Loop, the wife of one of Taylor's partners, who borrowed this name from Bayard Taylor's poem, "Paseo del Mar." Casa Del Mar Hotel was destroyed by fire in 1890. In 1887 Del Mar had a population of 300. (G.)

The elaborate 1912 sales brochure of South Coast Land Company declared:

> ...to offer to the man or woman of leisure and means, a real resting place by the sea, free from noise, confusion, and ugly cheap details of the average beach resort. Del Mar is planned for the exclusive.

DE LUZ: Town, Creek, Heights. According to local tradition an Englishman named Luce kept a corral of horses here, the site being referred to as Luce's corral. Spanish-speaking settlers pronounced it as "Corral de Luz." Establishment of a post office in 1882 shortened it to De Luz. (G.) (North from Fallbrook.)

Back county boom note of 1891: "It is reported trains will be running to De Luz in a few days." *(San Diego County Advertiser,* August 6, 1891.)

DESCANSO: Settlement, Valley. (Spanish for "rest" or "repose.") Local tradition reports that this place-name derives from the use of this settlement by land grant surveyors who stopped here regularly to eat their lunch in 1880. (Ha.)

DEVIL'S CANYON. A folk-name applied to two locations in the county: northeast from San Onofre, and southeast Anza-Borrego Desert. The name probably describes a forbidding aspect or special danger of passage for wagons and coaches. There are now 150 to 200 "Devil" name-places in California. (G.)

Devil's Jumpoff (Santa Ysabel) and Devil's Punch Bowl (El Capitan) denote homespun folk images of the Prince of Darkness.

DICK SPRING. Long-time resident Alice Bergman reported that this spring is on the ranch land east from Oak Grove that her parents once owned. The family had a favorite dog named Dick who slipped into the spring one day in a most amusing fashion. Thereupon they named the spring for their dog. (This is an excellent example of a folk-naming based on an event.)

DICTIONARY HILL. When is a dictionary not a dictionary? When it's an encyclopedia, of course. And thereby lingers a legend of a sort — about an elevation.

On February 21, 1911, the pompously named East San Diego Villa Heights was filed as a subdivision, located north from Sweetwater Lake and two and one-half miles southeast of La Mesa. Persons in the Midwest who purchased certain encyclopedia sets received a lot in the present "Dictionary Hill" as a premium. Somehow the word "dictionary" soon became a nickname substitute for "encyclopedia." Researcher John Davidson reported that the San Diego County surveyor of 1911 opposed this legal filing, for he announced to the public that the area lacked water — and therefore was uninhabitable.

One legend had it that the site was designated as Dictionary Hill since only such a book could contain all the superlatives the developers guaranteed it contained. Another legend reported that early Indians used this hill as a signal site.

According to John Davidson, most of these lots were eventually sold for delinquent taxes. (J.D., W.D.)

DILLON CANYON. An apparent personal name designation in Imperial Beach whose identity is not known.

DIVISION. An apt descriptive name for the place where the San Diego, Arizona, and Eastern Railroad once crossed the Mexican border into the U.S. about three miles south of Canyon City. (See also under HIPASS.)

DOANE: Lake, Valley. This personal place-name derives from George Doane, an early settler in the Palomar district. He was regarded as a romantic character who was inclined to propose to every single woman he met. Finally, he advertised for a wife, and a Georgia widow responded. Doane traveled to Georgia to meet her — but returned with the widow's 16-year-old daughter as his wife. (C. Wood, p. 59)

DODGE VALLEY. A personal place-name for F.E. Dodge who settled in the Oak Grove district in 1887 as a stockman. Broken in health, and given only one year to live, he came to the desert where he enjoyed a normal life for many years. "I even survived my doctor!" was his boast on his 70th birthday.

DOG SPRING. A folk-name possibly related to an incident that occurred here involving a dog. Gudde reports at least 25 "dog" place-name designations in California. (See also under COWLES MOUNTAIN.) (In Mission Valley.)

DONOHUE MOUNTAIN. A personal place-name designation for Stuart Donohue, an early settler and mine operator in the Dulzura district.

DON SPRING. No information is available for this personal place-name in Tubb Canyon. (See also under TUBB CANYON.)

DOS CABEZAS SPRING. (Spanish for "two heads.") The source of this intriguing name is two separated heaps of boulders above a spring that suggest a silhouette of two heads. (H. Parker, p. 78) This is a prominent land feature in Anza-Borrego Desert Park.

DOUBLE PEAK. A descriptive designation for a geographical formation in San Marcos district.

DRY: Canyon, Valley. Such a name designation often is a type of folk-and-descriptive-complaint. (Ranchita area.)

DUBBERS. G.W. Grosdidier, who worked for the San Diego, Arizona, and Eastern Railway during its construction, recalled this designation as the name of a civil engineer who also was employed by the railroad company. The site is north from Jacumba.

DULZURA: Settlement, Summit. (Spanish for "place of sweetness.") Local tradition reports that this name was proposed by resident Mrs. Hagenbeck, a devotee of wild flowers. The district was well known as a center for honey and milk production. Small amounts of gold were discovered here at the end of the nineteenth century. (G.)

DURASNITOS SPRING. (Spanish for "small peaches.") A descriptive name-designation for a location in Ramona district. Its name origin is not known.

DUTCHMAN CANYON. Dorothy Clark Schmid is a long-time resident in Dulzura district, and the author of an interesting local history, *Pioneering in Dulzura*. She was instrumental in preserving this nickname-designation for an early sheepherder who lived here before 1880.

The site was never marked on area maps. Mrs. Schmid's petition to the U.S. Board of Geographical Names in Washington, D.C., received official approval August 23, 1974, for Dutchman Canyon to be designated as a place-name on the county map.

DYCHE VALLEY. Named for a pioneer from Virginia, George Dyche, who settled in the Palomar district in 1868. Mrs. Dyche was of Indian origin. Dyche was cattle boss on Warner's Ranch before he pioneered the Palomar area. (J.D.)

DYE: Canyon, Mountain. Named for John Dye, pioneer settler from Kentucky who crossed the plains as a youth. Mr. Dye was the father of 13 children. (Located south from Ballena.) (J.D.)

EAGLE: Crag, Peak. Eagle Crag is one of the higher mountains in the northern part of the county, north from Pala. Eagle Peak is located southwest from Julian. (J.D.)

EAGLES NEST. The Indian place-name was "Aswanet" for "place of the eagle." It was anglicized by Hiram Keyes who homesteaded here with his wife in the 1880s. Their ranch land rose to an elevation of 5500 feet, so Keyes staked out his claim in a zigzag fashion in order to select the best soil. This resulted in a most irregular boundary line of his fruit and vegetable farm. Keyes and his wife operated a commercial summer camp, and weekly he drove a wagon to San Diego to pick up his guests. In this manner he was assured his guests would stay for at least a week. The ranch was located on Los Coyotes Reservation, about 5 miles east from Warner Springs. The ample supply of water and game in this immediate district was a great satisfaction to settlers and also to the earlier Indians. (J.D., Hu.)

Years later Col. Ed Fletcher purchased the ranch.

EARTHQUAKE VALLEY. *The San Diego Union,* April, 1971, reported:

> Residents are not sure how it was named. Many who reside here now do not like the name and call it Shelter Valley.

Earthquake Valley is located in Anza-Borrego Desert.

EAST BUTTE. This is a land feature in the Anza-Borrego area.

EAST FORK LIZARD CANYON. Such a double-barreled appellation is in proper order as a site in Earthquake Valley.

EASTWOOD: Creek, Hill. A possible personal place-name in the Julian area.

ECHO: Valley, Mountain. Located in the Barrett Valley area. This is a common type of name-feature throughout the U.S.

EDWARDS CREEK. A personal place-name whose identity is not known. (Located northeast from Clark Valley.)

EGG MOUNTAIN. Located west of Carrizo Badlands, this feature is a large oval-shaped heap of sand and vegetation. (Range Jack Welch)

EL CAJON: City, Mountain, Valley. (Spanish for "box" or "box-like canyon.") El Cajon's history began soon after the founding of Mission San Diego de Alcala in 1769. The need for extensive pasturage for the mission's sheep and cattle led the padres to the lush, grassy floor of El Cajon Valley — although the padres designated "Santa Monica" as its place-name. By 1795 the Mission owned 25,000 sheep and cattle in this pasturage. The Indian name for the district was "Amut-tar-tu," "level ground center."

San Diego County was the last Southern California county to abandon stock-raising as a livelihood. After 1870 some ranchers in this area began to experiment with the growing of fruits and vegetables. By 1885 it was commonly recognized in the county that agriculture had become the major ranch interest in El Cajon Valley.

The city of El Cajon is named for El Cajon Rancho, a land grant made in 1845 to Doña Maria Estudillo Pedrorena. Today's La Mesa, Grossmont, Bostonia, Santee, Lakeside, and Flinn Springs are part of this earlier Mexican land grant. The name of this town originally was written as "Elcajon." In 1905 the Post Office Department separated it as "El Cajon." (J.D., G., B.)

In 1974 El Cajon's population was the third largest in the county.

EL CAMINO REAL. (Spanish for "royal road.") Erwin Gudde states in *California Place Names:*

> In Spanish days *camino real, camino nacional* or *camino principal* designated the public roads and trails between presidios, missions, and settlements. The name is now applied to the modern highways connecting the missions and is often erroneously interpreted to mean the "king's highway." (p. 48)

EL CAPITAN RESERVOIR. (See under CAPITAN GRANDE.)

ELENA MOUNTAIN. An apparent personal place-name in Barrett Lake area that remains unexplained.

ELLA WASH. Park Ranger Jack Calvert named this site to honor his wife. Unusual sandstone patterns can be seen at this Borrego Badlands feature.

ELLIS SPRING. An apparent personal name whose identity is not known. (Alpine district.)

EL PRADO MEADOW. Since "prado" translates as "meadow," one suspects that a Yankee homesteader created this tautological place-name for a site on Monument Peak in the Laguna region.

ENCANTO. (Spanish for "charm" or "enchantment.") This descriptive place-name was bestowed on the southeast San Diego district in 1889 by Alice Klauber, whose family first developed this area. (Previously it had been known as Klauber Park.) She stated:

> I chose "Encanto" because of its salubrious climate and the views of the ocean and San Diego which it affords.

This choice of a Spanish form of name instead of an English one suggests the strength of Spanish culture that still existed in the county at this time.

In 1907 the Richard Realty Company offered to name a street for each purchaser of a 10-acre tract at this site. (J.D., B.)

ENCINITAS. (Spanish for "place of little oaks.") When the Portola expedition marched northward in search of Monterey, it entered a valley of small live oak trees two days after leaving San Diego. Father Crespi named this "Cañada de los Encinos." It is one of the few remaining place-names designated by Crespi and the Portola expedition. A land grant in 1842 was titled "Rancho de los Encinitas." However, the present town is not a parcel of the land grant.

The first settler here was Chicagoan Nathan Eaton who arrived in 1875. He kept bees, seemed to prefer a hermit's existence, and built the first house in this town — using old lumber with flattened tin cans for roof shingles. His brother was General C. Eaton of Civil War prominence.

Early biographical cameo:

> Eaton was a very picturesque figure. He had a wagon which consisted of 4 wheels and a shaky frame fastened together with bale rope (this was before the days of baling wire). Two little mules furnished the motive power. When one of them died, he pickled it and had 'corned beef' for many a day thereafter. . . .
>
> When the railroad came thru, Mr. Eaton built a house out of old boards and powder cans from the construction camp. The cans were cut down one side and opened out. When thus treated, they made excellent weather-proof shingles. . . .
>
> This is the man who started the Australian salt-bush in Southern California. He saw it advertised and sent to Australia for the seed. He kept his pockets full and scattered it over the country wherever he went with his mule team. He hoped that it would make good forage for cattle, but it has proved to be a nuisance wherever cultivation has taken place. *(The Coast Dispatch,* June 19, 1947, article by longtime resident Annie H. Cozzens.)

ENYEART CREEK. Apparently a personal name-designation that remains unexplained. (Located north from Warner Springs.)

ESCONDIDO: City, Creek. (Spanish for "hidden.") This descriptive place-name derives from the Anza expedition that camped at this creek which they referred to as "Agua Escondido." The city is in the center of the Mexican land grant of Rincon del Diablo (Devil's Corner) Rancho. The southern part of the city is on the old San Bernardo Rancho. (J.D.)

In 1885 a syndicate of Los Angeles and San Diego businessmen bought the Rincon del Diablo Rancho, laid out the town at a crossroads called Apex, and named the town after Escondido Creek. (G.)

1894 Back-County-Hustle-Bustle: "The Escondido gold mine now shows a 7-foot vein of paying rock." *(San Diego County Advertiser,* January 27, 1894.)

In 1974 Escondido ranked fifth in population in the county.

ESPINOSA CREEK. An apparent personal place-name in Barrett Lake district whose identity is unknown.

EUCALYPTUS HILLS. A descriptive place-name for a site located north from Lakeside. (See also under ROCKWOOD CANYON and under RANCHO SANTA FE.)

FAIRBANKS LAKE. This personal designation was for movie actor Douglas Fairbanks, Sr., who purchased 800 acres in 1926. He developed a country estate here which featured the cultivation of Valencia oranges. The lake, 5 miles east from Solana Beach, is named after the ranch. (J.D.) (See also under LUSARDI.)

FALLBROOK. This is a transferred or borrowed place-name designation of the original home town in Fallbrook, Pennsylvania, of early settler Vital Reche. He came here in 1858, successfully producing honey which he brand-named "Fallbrook." It must have been a popular brand in its day, for the brand name eventually became the place-name for the town. (B.)

The site once was a part of famous Santa Margarita Rancho. Although settler Reche provided the name, the place grew when developer Bartlett in 1882 purchased 160 acres and laid out most of the present town.

FARLEY FLAT. An apparent personal site designation in Descanso district. Its identity is not known.

FEATHERSTONE CANYON. David Stone, a resident in Julian, reported that several boulders in this canyon (Barona district) have prominent markings that suggest a crude feather pattern. Hence the canyon's descriptive appellation.

FERGUSON FLAT. An apparent personal place-name in Julian district whose identity remains unknown.

FERNBROOK. A descriptive designation for a settlement in Barona district.

FERN CREEK. This is in a canyon near De Luz, north from Fallbrook, noted for its scenery and attractive fern growth. (J.D.)

FILAREE FLAT. An unexplained name for a site on Monument Peak, near Mt. Laguna. (See also under MONUMENT PEAK.)

FIRE MOUNTAIN. Oceanside historian Ernest Taylor suggests that the red stone outcroppings on the slopes of this elevation may be the origin of this place-name. The elevation is south of Oceanside.

FISH CREEK: Mountain, Wash. Probably named for the marine fossils discovered here. This Anza-Borrego Desert creek is frequently explored by paleontologists. Its sandy wash served as an artery principally for prospectors and freighters who were familiar with the Badland district. Occasionally, greenhorn prospectors who ventured into this forbidding area never again were seen alive. Eastern San Diegueño Indians may have been speaking epitaphically if they casually remarked, "They went in but never came out." Local tradition had it that a site in the creek may have been an ancient Indian burial ground.

Horace Parker, authority on the Anza-Borrego Desert, considers the desert "one of California's last frontiers." Such an extraordinary geological region has had a blustering history: from earliest Indians to colonizing Spanish missionaries; from Mexican and Yankee gold-seekers to Civil War deserters and post-Civil War refugees; from desert adventurers and desperados to Yankee immigrants seeking a new and better way of life in Southern California. Yet the desert's exclusive geography remains as varied as its historical parade of primitives, *asistencias,* covered wagons, cattlemen, and desert prospectors.

Humanity has merely been an intruder in a place whose relentless perpetuity eventually dispelled his presence and function. (*Anza-Borrego Desert Guide,* p. 17)

FLINN SPRINGS. Named for James E. Flinn who first homesteaded as a young man at Corte Madera. He was said to have been a Confederate sympathizer who went south to Mexico to evade the draft. Flinn returned to San Diego in 1865 and carried mail on horseback before settling at Corte Madera. (See also under CORTE MADERA.)

The San Diego Union and Daily Bee, April 2, 1889, reported that Flinn and his family settled at this spring in the 1870s. The special quality of this water made it a popular stop for freight wagons and stages on the long journey between Yuma and San Diego. Today Flinn Springs, east from El Cajon, is a county park for picnickers. (Hu.)

Hogs for earlier Mission San Diego were raised in the area just west from these springs.

FLORES HILL. (See under LAS FLORES.)

FOLEY CANYON. An apparent personal name-place in San Onofre area whose identity remains unknown.

FONTS POINT. Padre Pedro Font was chaplain of the second Anza expedition (1775-1776). His diary and maps are valuable sources for early Spanish names. Font vividly described in his diary the awesome and terrifying view of Borrego Badlands as he stood at this elevation of 1294 feet. He stated that the mountains of rocks and boulders "look as if they had been brought and piled up there, like the sweepings of the world."

Although Font saw the Borrego Badlands as a kind of no man's land of lurking demons and gargoylish ghouls, desert authority Horace Parker characterized this kaleidoscopic phenomenon of erosion and desolation as "sculptured sediments of prehistoric lakes." Where Font may have imagined the appearance of a stygian inferno or medieval Hell, Horace Parker was fascinated by the forms and shapes of dry lake bottoms, winding washes, and intricate patterns of mud hills. (H. Parker, p. 33)

FORESTER CREEK. This unexplained place-name suggests a personal type of designation. (Alpine district.)

FORTUNA MOUNTAIN. Was this name-designation hopefully borrowed from the Greek goddess Fortuna? Its name origin remains unknown. (Located west from Santee.)

FOSS LAKE. In the San Luis Rey district, named for David Foss, a prominent merchant, farmer, and justice of the peace who came to this area in 1872.

FOUR CORNERS. This common Yankee name-description for a crossing of roads is for two such sites in the county: one is just east from San Vicente Mountain; the other is south from Los Piños Mountain.

FRANKS PEAK. The identity of this personal place-name remains unexplained. (Escondido district.)

FRED CANYON. An apparent personal place-name that remains unexplained. (Laguna district.)

FRENCH CANYON. Place-named for settlers of French origin. This designation is a nickname form. (Oceanside area.)

FREY CREEK. Long-time resident Marcus Galsh reported that George and John Frey homesteaded in Pala district before 1900. They were cattle-raisers and sizable bee-keepers.

GALETTA MEADOWS. A descriptive Spanish designation in Anza-Borrego district for a type of desert grass. (L. Reed, p. 59)

GALLOWAY VALLEY. An apparent and unexplained personal name in Alpine district.

GARLIC FLATS. The existence of strong-scented Allium plants in Valley Center district certainly suggested this descriptive or folk-type name designation on Rodriguez Mountain.

GARNET MOUNTAIN. A descriptive name for the garnet stones found in the higher peak area of Laguna Mountains. (B.)

This reddish glasslike mineral occurred in other parts of California where it also was applied as a place-name, an indication of its known value in earlier times.

GASKILL PEAK. Christopher B. Gaskill, born in England, came to this county in 1887, homesteading 420 acres on a mountain slope in Lawson Valley area. He was not related to the Gaskills of Campo who became famous as participants in a spectacular holdup in their store. (Hu.) (See also under CAMPO.)

GEM HILL. This is a generic yet descriptive place-name for the earlier prospecting and mining of tourmaline at this locale in Mesa Grande district.

GERT WASH. A dry stream bed in Carrizo Mountains. This name remains unexplained.

GHOST MOUNTAIN. A folk name whose origin is not known yet is extremely suggestive. (Earthquake Valley, Anza-Borrego Desert.)

GLENVIEW. Situated in El Cajon Valley and apparently name-designated for its descriptive location.

GOAT: Mountain, Peak. Goats were not native to California. Were imported herds of goats raised at Goat Mountain (Live Oak Springs) and on Goat Peak (Poway)? Was a lost or dead goat reported once at these sites?

GODFREY CREEK. The identity of this personal place-name possibly is that of Michael F. Godfrey, an Irish immigrant, who lived nearby about 1894. (Santee area.)

GOMEZ CREEK. An apparent personal place-name whose identity remains unknown. (Pala area.)

GONZALES CANYON. Del Mar resident Alice Goodkind reported that the canyon was named for Don Levi Gonzales, a rancher from Portugal, who cultivated fruit and nut trees. His wagon of fresh farm products was a frequent sight in the streets of Del Mar.

GOOSE VALLEY. This place-name turkey-trotted through slips of tongue that would delight a writer of newspaper headlines: A local lingering account is that of a Quaker group of settlers who homesteaded west of Santa Ysabel, naming their new home "El Valle de los Amigos." Mispronunciation or indifference shortened it to "Los'gos Valley." Later it became integrated to "Los Goose," and finally the apparent triumph of American usage made it "Goose Valley." (An amusing account, although without corroboration.) (J.D.)

GOPHER CANYON. Cave J. Couts Senior reported this place-name to be aptly descriptive. (Bonsall district.) (J.D.)

GOVERNMENT SPRINGS. Was this a name applied by — or for — government surveyors of earlier years? (Located north from Ranchita.)

GRANITE: Mountain, Springs. A descriptive name application for its granite composition. (Earthquake Valley area of Anza-Borrego district.)

GRAPEVINE: Creek, Spring, Mountain, Canyon. These descriptive land features designate the wild grapevines growing in various places in the county. At one time there were two canyons, two creeks, one spring, and a mountain with the designation of "Grapevine."

Grapevine Canyon (south from Ranchita) provided a meandering and twisting wagon passage through picturesque desert growth and hidden springs. Borrego State Park Ranger Alfred Welcome reported that many sought gold here unsuccessfully. And their disappointment did not deter later prospectors, for the "maybe" of a gold legend was much more alluring than the frenzied failures of earlier prospectors.

In his first letter from San Diego in 1769, Father Serra mentioned the abundance of wild grapevines in the surrounding arroyos. (J.D.)

GRAVE WASH. Although uncorroborated, such a folk-type place-name is quite self-explanatory. (Located east from Clark Valley near Imperial County line.)

GREEN VALLEY. This is a common descriptive California name designation, both in English and in Spanish (Valle Verde). Green Valley is located in Cuyamaca District.

In Elizabeth Johnson's *Indian Legends of the Cuyamacas* is the legendary Indian story of " Hilsh Ki′e and the Battle of the Peaks": A long time ago there were many, many peaks in Cuyamaca. There came a time when the peaks quarreled, all the peaks besieging Hilsh Kiê. They belched out huge rocks on his head. Hilsh Ki′e battled furiously, twisting the head of South Peak, leaving a crook in his neck forever. His struggle, however, was in vain, and he finally retreated, running away from his home.

> Exhausted at last, he fell in the midst of the low-browed mountains with short-cropped hair. And that is where you find him today — grand old Hilsh Ki′e (Pine Tree) with pine-topped crest and a ragged, jagged, rough-hewn scar where he broke off sharp from...Kwe-ah-mac′ (Water Beyond), — there among aliens far from his people. (p. 10)

(See also under CUYAMACA.)

GROSSMONT. This site was developed by Col. Ed. Fletcher and his actor-partner, William Gross, and place-named for the latter in 1900. Researcher Lena B. Hunzicker reported:

At the time of its purchase it was a barren and almost inaccessible mountain with huge boulders and many rattlesnakes. Previous to its development, a railroad station close by was known as "Alta." The transformation of this place was brought about by many miles of winding roads that lead to the summit.

The site was to be a colony for artists, and so it eventually became. Among the first home-builders were Madame Schumann-Heink, singer Carrie Jacobs Bond, poet John Vance Cheney, critic Havrah Hubbard, and novelist Owen Wister. Other famous singers and musicians of the day later owned homes here.

"Fletcher's Folly" was the derisive name among San Diego realtors for Fletcher's difficulties with road-building. A La Mesa newspaper mockingly printed in bold, black headlines: "F.F.F.F.: Freaky Fletcher's Fancy Flight."

Carrie Jacobs Bond described her sentiments about Grossmont in her poem, "A Cottage in God's Garden":

There's a cottage in God's Garden,
Upon a mountain high,
Away from strife and turmoil
And all life's din and cry.
Away from care and sorrow,
From all life's tears and woe,
A cottage in God's garden
Where I am free to go.

There's a cottage in God's garden
Where my tired feet may rest
And weary though my soul may be,
My spirit there be blessed.
The wild birds chant their carols,
The flowers bloom galore
Out in God's lovely garden —
How could I ask for more?

GUAJOME LAKE. A descriptive Indian designation for "place of the frog," located on the Mexican land grant Guajome Rancho. The grant was given to Indian neophytes Andres and Caterina Solma in 1845. It was later sold to businessman Abel Stearns of Los Angeles for $550. In 1851 Stearns presented the ranch to Lt. Cave Johnson Couts and his wife (Isidora Bandini) as a wedding present. Couts soon built one of the most extensive haciendas in the county, using adobe, tile, and timber in a manner that has stood the test of time for over a century. Lt. Couts also owned the nearby San Marcos Rancho. (P. Rush, pp. 18-20)

Helen Hunt Jackson described Guajome in her novel, *Ramona.*

GUATAY: Town, Mountain. An Indian descriptive designation signifying "large rock." The valley here was a favorite wintering locale for the Cuyamaca Indians, who summered in the higher mountains where they gathered acorns and seeds before the coming of winter storms. Above this valley was large Guatay Mountain which was thought to be the home of a great chief. These Indians kept their ancient religion and customs, remaining untouched by any mission influence. When Mexican and American homesteaders came here in the 1850s they encountered a large population of natives. (Ha., Rensch)

Mary Elizabeth Johnson's *Indian Legends of the Cuyamacas* retells the superstitious legend of Na-wa Ti´e (Big House or Guataj), "the mountain that appears as a large wigwam from any point of view."

> Then the comely Indian maids, pounding their acorn meal in the Hamoo-ka´e (mortars) on the rocky knoll of the village, were fearful of incurring the displeasure of Na-wa Ti´e (Big House). Even the valiant warriors, brave in their fierce array, dared not ascend the mountain side, or pluck one branch of the rare trees growing there. Eel-sha-har´ (Grows Only Here) they called them.

> For to Na-wa Ti´e (Big House), was given the power of creating the penetrating wind, the blighting frost, the freezing snow, and the driving sleet. When enraged it caused the spirit of Ha-choor´ (Cold) to spring out from the center of its heart chilling the marrow of their bones, and carrying devastation throughout the fertile valley.

So one and all gazed on it with awe; molesting it not, never venturing up its slopes; ever fearful, ever dreading, lest they might arouse the ire of Na-wa Ti´e (Big House). (pp. 16-17)

GUEJITO: Creek, Settlement. (Spanish for "small gravel.") This creek and ranchito (north from San Pasqual) were located on the earlier Guejito Rancho, a Mexican land grant awarded to Jose Maria Orozco in 1845. R.W. Brackett's *History of San Diego County Ranches* stated:

> In 1843 Orozco was alternate justice of the peace and collector of customs in San Diego. . . .During the war of 1846 Orozco sided with the Mexican forces; it was he who fired upon Albert B. Smith as the latter climbed the flag pole at Old Town to reeve new halyards for the American flag. Bancroft says that Orozco also amused himself by shooting at Miguel de Pedrorena merely to frighten him while the latter was escorting a young lady. (p. 54.)

Indian pictographs once existed nearby. (J.D.)

HALFHILL DRY LAKE. An uncommon place-name in Borrego Desert that remains unexplained.

HAPAHA FLAT. An Indian place-name for Carrizo Gorge in Anza-Borrego Desert. It appeared earlier as "Hapawa," signifying "reed, cane, or coarse grass." (J.D.)

The Indians in this district were known as "Kamias" or Eastern Diegueños. They were largely a seed-gathering and hunting people. It is reported that their pottery, articles of personal adornment, and beads were simple and crude, probably due to their preoccupation with food-gathering. However, their small arrowheads are considered to be of superior quality.

HARBISON CANYON. Designated after John Harbison, pioneer and innovative bee-keeper, who homesteaded in this canyon in 1869 with a choice collection of 110 bee hives. One year he shipped over 200,000 pounds of honey to Eastern markets. He is honored as the founder and "father" of the honey business in southern California. During his career, when other area ranchers had also taken up bee-keeping, San Diego County became the leader in the U.S. for honey production.

The Indian name for this canyon (west from Alpine), "Ha-nu-way," remains unexplained. (J.D., B.)

HARMONY GROVE. A descriptive place-name in Escondido district so designated for its pleasant surroundings. It was nicknamed "Spook Canyon" because of the annual meetings held here by spiritualist groups. Erwin Gudde reports "Harmony" as a place-name in 24 communities in 1868 all over the U.S., a unique popularity for a place-name resulting from the end of the Civil War. (J.D., G.)

This district at one time contained mortars, metates, pictographs, and petroglyphs, all ample evidence of extensive earlier Indian activity. (J.D.)

HARPER: Canyon, Flat, Creek. Place-named for brothers Julius and Amby Harper whose fine herd of Durham cattle was envied by other cattlemen in the district. They fattened their beef cattle in Pinyon Mountain area and then shipped them to market from Temecula. (L. Reed, pp. 63-64)

HATFIELD CREEK. Named for a homesteader in Ramona area whose descendant was Charles M. Hatfield of rainmaking fame in San Diego County history. (J.D.)

HAUSER CANYON. Designated after a pioneer in Moreno reservoir district who settled here soon after the Civil War. (J.D.)

HAWK CANYON. A descriptive and folk place-name for a site at Borrego Mountain.

HELL CREEK. Jack Schmid, resident in Pauma Valley, reported the following explanation of this folk-name: Travelers had to cross the creek on their journey from Palomar to Escondido. Frequent floodings made it very difficult for wagons to ford the stream. The name "Hell Creek" must be regarded as a folk-fossil of frustration and mild profanity.

HELLHOLE: Canyon, Flat. A folk place-name for a narrow abrupt canyon leading from Montezuma Valley into Borrego Valley. Cattleman William Johnson Helm once declared it was "one hell of a job to get wild cattle out of it," and thereafter he always referred to it as "Hellhole Canyon."

Early population note: At age 75, cattleman Helm became the father of twins. (J.D.)

HENDERSON CANYON. This personal place-name for a site north from Borrego Springs was for Dave Henderson, a mining engineer in Julian district. Born in California, he later graduated from Oxford University in Great Britain. His career included travels to China, Africa, Australia, Peru, and Canada as a mining consultant.

HIDDEN GLEN. A descriptive place-name in Lawson Valley, northeast from Jamul.

HIDDEN SPRINGS. An aptly descriptive name designation in Anza-Borrego Desert for an important water source for prospectors – and certainly for the earlier Indians. (J.D.)

HIDEAWAY LAKE. Such a descriptive place-name seems to testify to what its location significantly provided. (Valley Center area.)

HIGHLAND VALLEY. A descriptive name-place of an area of higher ground in the San Pasqual district.

HIGH POINT. A place-name for the highest point on Mt. Palomar; its Indian counterpart was "Wikyo." The Palomar observatory was erected here at 5580 feet elevation, and High Point, an unforested peak, is at 6126 feet elevation. (C. Wood)

HILL VALLEY. A descriptive name designation about 4 miles west from Boulevard.

HIPASS. An elevation of 3660 feet, this name designation is a coined form of name for "high pass." It was the highest point on the San Diego, Arizona, and Eastern Railroad.

The S.D.A. and E. was the last railroad built (1919) to link the Pacific Coast with the Eastern states. It was designed to connect San Diego, a deepwater port, with El Centro and Yuma in Imperial Valley. The railroad was 148 miles long. At one point it passed through Baja California in order to avoid the San Ysidro Mountains. It made its final passenger run on January 11, 1951.

This district was earlier referred to simply as "Indian country." (J.D.) In 1956 the post office name "Hipass" was changed to "Tierra del Sol." (G.)

HOLLENBECK CANYON. A personal place-name whose identity remains unexplained. (Dulzura district.)

HORNO: Canyon, Hill. (Spanish for "oven" or "kiln.") Was this possibly a name designation that referred to its temperature which was unbearably hot at times? (Located south from San Onofre.)

HORSETHIEF CANYON. During the 1870s and 80s this site was used by horse thieves to hide stolen horses in preparation for their sale on the Mexican side of the border. Hence this place-name. (J.D.)

The canyon's narrow wall formed a natural corral, it had a water supply, and was quite secluded. (North from Barrett Lake.)

HOT SPRINGS MOUNTAIN. In earlier days this descriptive designation northeast from Warner Springs was known as "Agua Caliente" (hot or warm water), indicating early Spanish or Mexican settlers in the district. Eventually it was anglicized by later Yankee homesteaders.(B.)

HUBBARD SPRING. An apparent personal form of place-name whose identity remains unexplained. (Located southwest from Dulzura.)

IMPERIAL BEACH. Before California became part of the United States, the Imperial Beach area was a parcel of the extensive land holdings of Don Santiago Arguello, who once owned all the land from the tip of San Diego Bay to the Mexican border.

"Imperial Beach" was place-named by E.W. Peterson, manager of the South San Diego Investment Company, in order to appeal to Imperial Valley residents to build summer homes on the beach. A company newspaper ad offered "waterfront lots at $25 down and $25 monthly." Another developer's brochure claimed the balmy, soothing climate would "cure rheumatic proclivities, catarrhal trouble, lesions of the lungs," and a wide assortment of other ailments. (Ha., G.)

Originally this site was referred to as "South San Diego." In 1974 Imperial Beach ranked tenth in population in the county.

Historical boom days memo: *The San Diego County Advertiser,* July 15, 1891, reported the development of South San Diego district:

The 'head of the bay country' is fast becoming the Oakland of San Diego. Many of the citizens do business in the city, and at the same time are improving ranch homes in this beautiful district. Among these are Sheriff Folks and Deputy, County Surveyor Allen, besides lawyers, doctors, and preachers.

INAJA INDIAN RESERVATION. A small reservation located about 8 miles south from Julian whose 840 acres had been used mainly for grazing. Only a small portion of the reservation was irrigated or could be used for dry farming. Its locale is quite scenic. Reasonable amounts of game are still present, with hunting privileges reserved for the Indians. Thirty-four Indians were reported living here in 1933. An article in *The San Diego Union,* January 23, 1972, reported no Indians in residence.

(For its name derivation see under ANAHUAC.)

INDIAN: Springs, Hill, Gorge, Canyon, Creek, Dam Flats, Head, Hill, Potrero, Rock, Corral, Valley. This cluster place-name was frequently applied to places of earlier Indian campsites, or to places where federal surveyors found significant settlement of Indians in the immediate area of survey. Occasionally, "Indian" was a folk-form of name related to an event that involved settlers directly. Quite often it was applied with a derogatory intention.

Indian Springs, just west from Jamul, was established and named by Mr. and Mrs. Honnell in 1919. They built a museum of Indian relics which they managed until 1936. Manifestly, this district once had been extensively used by Indians. (J.D.)

IN-KO-PAH. (Indian for "place of mountain people.") A place-name designated by highway surveyors to preserve the name of the Indians who once lived here. (B.) (Located in extreme southeast of the county.)

JACKASS FLAT. This Anza-Borrego location was a favorite resting place for wild burros. (Range Jack Welch)

JACUMBA: Town, Mountains. This preserved Indian place-name possibly signifies "hut by the water." It was first homesteaded by the McClain family, who came from Texas in a prairie schooner before the Civil War. (J.D.)

Of the Indians in the district *The San Diego Herald*, June 10, 1851, reported:

> The Indians here are spread over the valley and seemed to be in considerable numbers; they were kindly disposed; cultivate the earth to some extent; many have been into the settlements and talked a little Spanish.

Jacumba is just a tomahawk's throw from the Mexican border. It is one of the oldest inhabited sites in the county.

JAMACHA JUNCTION. Scholars do not agree on the meaning of this Indian place-name: One declares "small squash plant," and another states "gourd or mock orange." It was spelled variously as "Jamacho," "Hamacha," Jamoche," and "Gamacha." It is located south from El Cajon.

It is believed that some of the rebellious Indians who destroyed San Diego Mission November 4, 1775, and massacred Father Jaume, came from Jamacha.

The legendary yet elusive Pegleg mine was believed to be nearby. (J.D., Ha.)

JAMUL: Town, Butte, Creek, Mountains, Valley. The meaning of this Indian place-name southeast from Spring Valley has been variously declared as "slimy water," "place where antelope drink water," and "foam or lather." The records of San Diego Mission indicated it often used Jamul as a sheep pasturage. (J.D.)

JAPACHA PEAK. "Japacha" and "Jepeche" Indian *rancherias* (villages) are listed in mission records. However, its meaning remains unknown. (C. Hart Merriam, *Village Names of Twelve California Mission Records,* p. 162.) (Located south from Cuyamaca Reservoir.)

JAPATUL VALLEY. An Indian place-name that signifies either "place of water" or "fruit of the prickly pear," according to Phil Hanna and Erwin Gudde. An established Indian village called "Japatai" existed here until 1890. (G., Ha.) (Southeast from Alpine.)

JARDINE CANYON. An apparent personal place-name whose identity remains unexplained. (Camp Pendleton area.)

JESMOND DENE. Long-time Escondido resident Frances Ryan reported that subdividers named this place after the northern section of the city of Newcastle-on-Tyne in England.

JEWELL VALLEY. An apparent personal name designation whose identity remains unknown. (Jacumba district.)

JOFEGAN. Long-time Oceanside resident Vincent McGlenn was once an agent for the Santa Fe R.R. He recalled that this name designation was for Gen. Joseph Fegan, the first Camp Pendleton commander. The site was earlier known as "Stock Pen," serving as a cattle shipping station for the huge O'Neill Ranch (originally Rancho Santa Margarita y Las Flores). O'Neill Ranch was purchased by the U.S. Navy in 1942, and the present Camp Pendleton Marine Base was established.

Mr. McGlenn reported that the Stock Pen freight siding was a part of the original railroad line from San Diego to Chicago. It was enlarged in 1942 to accommodate trainloads of arriving Marines.

Statistical note: Camp Pendleton contains 5 lakes, 3 streams, 3 mountain areas, 260 miles of roadway, over 400 miles of enclosure fences, and several flagstone and granite quarries. (P.W. Brackett, p. 37) (See also under CAMP PENDLETON and SANTA MARGARITA.)

JOHNSON CANYON. Long-time resident Mrs. Claudell Klueber reported she and her husband purchased part of the Johnson Ranch in Otay district right after World War I. The Johnsons were two bachelor brothers who were regarded as eccentrics by other homesteaders. Mrs. Kleuber stated that the Johnsons maintained themselves in a very reclusive fashion.

JOY MEADOW. The probabilities and realities of such a folk-name's origin are anybody's interpretation. (Laguna district.)

JULIAN. Place-named for Mike Julian, mining recorder for the gold camp that was established here soon after the discovery of the George Washington gold mine in 1870. The townsite was laid out by Drury Bailey, Mike Julian's cousin. When asked why Bailey didn't designate his own name, he replied that "Julian" was more euphonious, that Mike was the handsomest man in town and a ladies' favorite, and that this place-name was a family honor since Mike was his cousin.

For a short time the town of Julian became the "Cinderella" of the county, and narrowly lost out on a vote to make it the county seat. Soon after 1900 ore-gold production waned. But then began a period of "green" gold: Julian proved to be an ideal district for deciduous fruit, especially as an apple-growing center. Apple and wildflower festivals have been annual events of great county interest and attendance, the first Apple Day occurring in 1909 and the first wildflower show in 1926. (J.D., W.D.)

Mining "namania" note: names of mines in gold-rush days ranged from the mundane to conceit, humor, or hope: Point Loma, Banner, Gold Beef, Red Rooster, Little Joker, Poor Man, Julian Dandy, Gold Monster, Shoo Fly, Hidden Treasure, Three Brothers, Gypsie, Mergold, Don't Bother Me, Maid of Texas, Last Chance, Square and Compass, April Fool, Tom Paine, and Afterthought. At least 15 percent of these mines were named after females: Martha, Dora, Laura, Ruby, Ella, Bertha, etc. (a yearning for womenfolk back home?)

KEYS (KEYES): Canyon, Creek. A personal place-name whose identity remains unexplained. (San Luis Rey District.)

KING CREEK. An apparent personal name-form whose identity remains unknown. (El Capitan region.)

KITCHEN: Creek, Valley. Named for Augustus Caesar Kitching (sic), an early cattleman from Texas. *The San Diego Union,* January 16, 1877, reported that Kitching had 30 acres of barley, 9 horses, and 3500 sheep in the valley. (Mt. Laguna district.) (J.D.)

1891 Back county boom statistics (from County Assessor's lists):			
Sheep and Lambs	28,372	Jacks, Jennies, and	
Stock Cattle	30,633	Mules	597
Milch Cows	3,919	Beehives	14,183
Horses and Colts	10,956	Poultry	30,624
Hogs	4,145	Ostriches (feather-	
		producing)	30

San Diego County Advertiser, July 25, 1891.

KLONDIKE CREEK. Obviously a transferred or borrowed name indicating the possible expression of irony — for a place too hot? too cold? or of no gold? The creek is south from Ramona.

LA COSTA. (Spanish for "the coast.") A pleasant-sounding descriptive name for a location near Batequitos Lagoon. Oliver H. Borden and his family were the first homesteaders in 1879. The county's first concrete house, north from the lagoon, was probably built by Borden. *The San Diego Union,* August 27, 1887, reported the presence of a threshing machine in this vicinity, making its rounds on the southern Pacific Coast for the first time. (E.B. Scott, p. 28)

Boom-town-days memo: The *San Diego County Advertiser* reported on September 24, 1891:

La Costa, the new railroad shipping point on the Metcalf place, is doing a thriving business.

La Costa post office was granted in 1896 but discontinued in 1905.

LAGO DE VIEJAS. (Spanish for "lake of the old women.") Tradition had it that an early Spanish expedition referred to an Indian village here as "Valle de las Viejas" because at the expedition's approach the natives fled, leaving behind only the old women. A Mexican land grant to Ramon and Leandro Osuna in 1846 established Rancho del Valle de las Viejas. A description of this period declared this district a superior grain-growing section of the county. (G.) (Alpine district.)

LAGUNA: Mountains, Summit. (Spanish for "lake" or "lagoon.") The origin of this place-name remains undisclosed. However, it designates an attractive and extensive public recreational area in California, located in Cleveland National Forest, and established by the U.S. Forest Service. (Ha.)

Gudde reports at least 30 "Laguna" designations throughout California.

LA JOLLA: Community, Indian Reservation. Much confusion and uncertainty exist concerning the place-name of this attractive coastal community. It has been variously declared by some to mean "pool"; by others to be from "hoya" (a hollow surrounded by hills); and by others as a possible corruption of "joya," Spanish for "jewel." (J.D.)

Nellie Van de Grift Sanchez in *Spanish and Indian Name Places of California* wrote:

> There is always the possibility that La Jolla means nothing of these, but is a corruption of some Indian word with a totally different meaning. More than one place in the state masquerades under an apparently Spanish name which is in reality an Indian word corrupted into some Spanish word to which it bore an accidental resemblance. (J.D., Hu.)

La Jolla Indian Reservation (Palomar district) was patented to the tribe in 1892, and had an area of 8,227 acres. It was estimated to have 23 residents in 1972.

A section of La Jolla Indian Reservation was once known as "Cuca Rancho." (The rancho originally was located at the foot of the western slope of Mt. Palomar, approximately twenty-five miles inland.)

The origin and meaning of "Cuca" is uncertain. One source declared it to be a Spanish word for "a root used as a coffee substitute." Long-time resident Abe Rodriguez of Valley Center district reported "Cuca" to be an Indian word whose meaning he could not recall. Rodriguez is a descendant of Gregorio Trujillo, a Luiseño Indian who married a descendant of the original grantee of Cuca Rancho. The land grant was made in 1845 to Maria Juana de Los Angeles.

Apparently the place-name of "Cuca" lingered long after it became a part of the La Jolla Indian Reservation, being variously spelled as "Kuka," "Kuki," and even "Caqui." (J.D., N. Green, P. Rush, pp. 72-74)

(See also under CUTCA VALLEY and RODRIGUEZ MOUNTAIN.)

LAKE DOMINGO. (Spanish for "Lord's day" or "Sunday.") Was this geographical feature (near Boundary Peak) once a popular Sunday recreational spot for homesteaders from either side of the Mexican border?

LAKE HENSHAW. A personal place-name for William G. Henshaw, a prominent promoter of water developments in the county. The irrigation reservoir is on the upper San Luis Rey River and was created in 1924. Rocks on the county road east of the lake once bore faint remains of Indian pictographs. (B., J.D.)

LAKE HODGES. A personal name-designation for W.E. Hodges, vice-president of Santa Fe Railroad. The lake extends almost to Escondido. (B., J.D.)

LAKE JEAN. A small lake on the present property of the Donato family at Sunshine Summit. Mr. Donato honored his wife when he designated this site Lake Jean.

LAKE SAN MARCOS. (See under SAN MARCOS.)

LAKESIDE. A descriptive place-name designated by the El Cajon Valley Company that laid out a townside of 3000 acres in 1887 on the western shore of Lake Lindo. James Jasper in *The Silver Gate Magazine,* January 1900, glowingly wrote:

> Picturesque Lakeside. . .in defiance of the ravages of the busted boom, and taxes, she has never yet acknowledged a superior in all southern California. Gentle reader, come with me to its vineclad verandahs and drink in the beauties of art and nature while I attempt to paint its pen-picture. . . .(p. 9)

LAKE VAL SERENO. (Spanish for "serene valley.") A descriptive name-designation whose derivation is unknown. (Olivenhain area.)

LAKE WOHLFORD. A personal place-name designated in 1924 for Alvin W. Wohlford, a banker and citrus grower who was prominent in the development of a water supply for the area. The first dam here, built in 1890, was merely a rock-fill with redwood facing; it was named Bear Valley Reservoir. Later it was name-changed to Escondido Lake — until 1924.

It was the policy of the county water authorities to name a reservoir after the person who was most influential in promoting such a created water supply. (J.D.)

LA MESA. (Spanish for "table land.") This is a descriptive place-name for its geographical location. Originally it was a Mexican land grant, and was considered an excellent grazing district. An artesian spring attracted Robert Allison, who developed a 4200-acre ranch here. Soon the place was referred to as "Allison Springs." In 1894 a townsite was laid out as "La Mesa Springs." In 1904 this was shortened to just "La Mesa." The construction of an aqueduct in 1889 to bring water from Cuyamaca Lake transformed the district from sheep-raising to the growing of citrus and avocado. (The present Spring Street in La Mesa is a reminder that the artesian spring was near the corner of La Mesa Boulevard and Spring Street.) (Hu.)

Theodore S. Van Dyke, who laid out the aqueduct system, later wrote in *The City and County of San Diego* regarding the need for water and cultivation:

> If ever a country needed good plowing it was San Diego County. If ever a country failed to get it, it was this same San Diego. The long tramp, tramp, tramp, of immense bands of sheep over the ground while it was wet had packed it to the hardness of an adobe brick. Even the alfileria and burr-clover which endured more ill treatment than almost any other vegetation, failed to reach half their natural size. . . .The desolate appearance given the land by the bands of sheep can scarcely be imagined today by those who look only upon the cultivated vineyards of El Cajon, or the alfalfa fields of San Jacinto. (p. 13)

In 1974 La Mesa had a population of more than 45,000, the sixth largest in the county.

LANCASTER MOUNTAIN. Long-time resident Jim Yarger recalled that the Lancaster family homesteaded at the foot of this mountain about 1890. (Located in San Luis Rey region.)

LA POSTA: Town, Creek, Indian Reservation. (Spanish for "relay stage or post.") This is the Spanish name for an Indian settlement named "Amai-tu" (meaning unknown). There once was a San Diego-Yuma stage relay station at the Cameron Valley settlement of La Posta. The reservation is just east of the town, an area of 3,879 acres, and was patented to the Indians in 1893. *The San*

Diego Union of January 23, 1972, reported no Indians in residence on the reservation. (J.D.)

LA PRESA. (Spanish for "dam.") An attractive mesa northeast of Sweetwater Dam, descriptively named for its location close to the dam. The townsite was laid out in 1887 by the San Diego Development Company. It was an immediate success as a San Diego suburb since it offered easy access to the city by train. *The Golden Era,* November, 1888, reported a schedule of "four trains daily each way." *(National City Record,* May 2, 1889.)

LARK CANYON. Anza-Borrego State Park Ranger Alfred Welcome reported this canyon to be an attractive scenic site. Further: local tradition regarded this site as a good place "to go and have a lark."

LAS FLORES. (Spanish for "flowers.") The Portola expedition camped nearby in 1769, naming it "Santa Praxedis de los Rosales" (Saint Praxedes of the Roses). Crespi wrote that the spot "was full of grapevines and innumerable castilian rosebushes and other flowers." An Indian pueblo began here in 1835. As a large native settlement, it later came under the jurisdiction of San Luis Rey Mission. After secularization, this pueblo became a part of the famous Santa Margarita y Las Flores ranch. As late as 1929 ruins of Indian adobes could still be seen here. (Ha., Hu.)

LAS PULGAS CANYON. (Spanish for "fleas.") These pesky insects were often encountered when the Portola expedition went north, for the soldiers nicknamed a deserted Indian village "Rancheria de las Pulgas." The mention of fleas or "pulgas" appears repeatedly in diaries and journals throughout the nineteenth century.

This canyon served as a pasture land for cattle of the San Luis Rey Mission. (J.D.)

LAWSON: Creek, Peak, Valley. Named for I.J. Lawson, an early pioneer in this district in the 1870s. (Located northeast from Jamul.) (J.D.)

LEE VALLEY. Named for an early settler in this district of Jamul. (Hu.)

LEMON GROVE. Descriptively named by the Allison brothers who were convinced this area was perfect for lemon cultivation. They laid out the townsite into 10-acre and 20-acre plots, water being available by flume from La Mesa. By 1893 many tracts had been sold to Eastern homeseekers.

During the 1880s the growth and use of lemons showed a considerable increase, for the new railroad now could ship lemons to eastern markets. In 1895 more than half the total planted acreage in the county comprised lemons. Suddenly San Diego County became California's leading lemon district. It was said that the back country was "a sea of lemon trees."

Lemon Grove is situated on original San Diego Mission pasturage land, and grazing land it remained until the Allison brothers changed its use. Because of its attractiveness, it was nicknamed "The Pasadena of San Diego County." (J.D.)

LEUCADIA. (Greek for "sheltered place.") According to an article in *The San Dieguito Citizen,* July 30, 1959, this community was developed and named by a group of British spiritualists who came to the U.S. seeking religious freedom. Having a predilection for ancient classical culture, they applied Greek and Roman names to all their streets: Hermes, Hygeia, Glaucus, Eolus, Hymettus, Orpheus, Vulcan, etc.

Leucadia is a transferred or borrowed name from a Greek Ionian island renowned for its olive oil, currants, and wine. (Ha., J.D.)

LILAC. The ceanothus (California lilac) grew in abundance in this part of San Luis Rey district, hence its name-designation. (J.D.)

LILLIAN HILL. An apparent personal place-name in Tule Springs district.

LION CREEK. A frequent place-name for some kind of event involving a mountain lion. (Palomar area.)

LITTLE BLAIR VALLEY. (See under BLAIR.)

LITTLE CEDAR CANYON. (See under CEDAR.)

LITTLE CLARK DRY LAKE. (See under CLARK.)

LITTLE LAGUNA LAKE. (See under LAGUNA.)

LITTLE LIBBY LAKE. In 1868 William and Catherine Libby, migrating to California from Maine, homesteaded at this lake in Oceanside district. Mr. Libby soon became a prominent dairyman. Descendants of the Libby family still reside on a portion of the original Libby property.

LITTLE TECATE PEAK. (See under TECATE.)

LIVE OAK SPRINGS. A descriptive place-name for a small cabin resort in the mountain adjacent to Campo Indian Reservation, settled by Charles Hill in 1886. (J.D.)

LIZARD CANYON. A descriptive place-name for a canyon in Yaqui Wildlife area, Anza-Borrego Desert.

LOMA ALTA CREEK. (Spanish for "higher hill.") Was this descriptive place-name to indicate a truly, really high hill? Or to designate it as the highest of low hills in this immediate area? (Located east from Oceanside.)

LONE FIR POINT. A descriptive place-name in Palomar district.

LONG CANYON. A descriptive name-form for a long and narrow canyon in Pine Valley district. The valley and peak nearby are named after the canyon. Another "Long Canyon" in the Laguna region remains unexplained. (B.)

"Long" was a frequent adjective for place-names, and Erwin Gudde reports there are more than 100 place-names of this form throughout California.

LONG POTRERO. (See under POTRERO.)

LOS COYOTES INDIAN RESERVATION. By the year 1917, twenty-eight reservations for Indians had been set apart in the southern part of California, and Los Coyotes was one of these. Its name was applied by the Spanish to the Diegueño Indians living in what is now known as Collins Valley in Borrego desert. No explanation of its name-designation is available. This Indian reservation is mentioned in Helen Hunt Jackson's *A Century of Dishonor.*

In *The Journal of Lt. Thomas Sweeny 1849-1853,* Sweeny wrote the following report:

> The Diegueño village of Cañada de los Coyotes. . .debouches into the upper end of Borrego Valley. The troops attacked the rebellious Indians on December 21, 1851. The tribesmen stood the first fire, but soon broke and scattered on the hillsides. Later many of them surrendered, and on Christmas morning the men celebrated the holiday by executing four of the Indian leaders. The condemned men knelt at the heads of their graves and a well directed volley tumbled them in. (p. 241)

The San Diego Union of January 23, 1972, reported 42 Cahuila Indian residents on this reservation, a mountainous district with not much farm land. (See also under SWEENEY PASS.)

LOS PEÑASQUITOS: Creek, Canyon. The meaning of this place-name is varied, one scholar reporting it as "small, round rocks," and another as "place of little cliffs." As a land grant of 1832, it became titled "El Rancho de Santa Maria de los Peñasquitos." (J.D., Ha.)

Tradition has it that grantee Ruiz planted and cultivated the first pear trees of the district. Rancho

Peñasquitos was the first privately owned ranch in the county. (P. Rush, p. 24)

Ruiz deeded his land to Francisco Maria Alvarado of San Diego in 1837, but Alvarado's claim was denied until 1873. Meanwhile, dashing Captain George Johnson married Alvarado's daughter and the captain became manager of the rancho. Johnson raced horses at Sacramento, sailed up and down the coast, and became one of the owners of the Colorado Navigation Company. In 1859 he wrote his affluent father in New York:

> I am begging to get married in June to a young lady in San Diego, Miss Estefana Alvarado, a niece of Don Pio Pico, the former Governor. . . .she speaks and writes English very well. . . .I am satisfied she will make me a good wife.

When they married, Johnson was 34 years old, and she was 19.

LOS PIÑOS MOUNTAINS. (Spanish for "pines.") A descriptive designation located north from Morena Reservoir. According to Erwin Gudde:

> The wealth of native pines in California made this tree the most popular for place naming, even in Spanish times. The name was repeatedly used by explorers who were struck by the pine-covered mountains and promontories after their passage along the treeless shores of Lower California. (p. 234)

LOS TULES. (Aztec for "water reeds.") An Aztec descriptive designation for a place which supplied cane or reeds that the Indians used to build their *wickiups* (shelters). This marshy area is adjacent to Warner Springs. (B.) (See also under TULE.)

LOST VALLEY. This ominous folk-name seems to suggest a tragic or fatal human experience. However, it was reported that Jim Stone of Mesa Grande applied this name in the 1880s because of the valley's inaccessibility and isolation. This valley, near Warner Springs, has been considered one of the county's wildest areas, accessible only by mere rough trails. (J.D.)

Historical note: Lost Valley served as a pasturage in the 1880s for Agua Caliente Indians, according to Helen Hunt Jackson's *A Century of Dishonor:*

> These Indians have in use another valley called Lost Valley, some fifteen miles from their village high up in the mountains, and reached only by one very steep trail. Here they keep their stock, being no longer able to pasture it below. They were touchingly anxious to have us write down the numbers of cattle, horses, sheep each man had, and report to Washington that the President might see how they were all trying to work. There are probably from one hundred and twenty-five to one hundred and fifty head of cattle owned in the village, about fifty horses, and one hundred sheep. (p. 487)

LOVELAND RESERVOIR. Named for Fremont Loveland, son of an early California pioneer. Mr. Loveland was a prosperous and prominent citizen of San Luis Rey district.

LUSARDI CREEK. Named for Peter Lusardi, an Italian immigrant who owned a ranch near the present Fairbanks Lake. He came to California as a gold seeker and later settled in the county in 1872. Douglas Fairbanks, Sr., purchased Lusardi ranch, renaming it "Rancho Zorro" to commemorate the movie that made "Zorro" a household word around the world. (J.D.) (See under FAIRBANKS LAKE.)

LYONS PEAK. Designated for General Nathaniel Lyons who was stationed in San Diego in the early 1850s. Highly esteemed, the general owned a parcel of land at the foot of this Jamul district mountain that was later named for him. History credits General Lyons with having influenced the state of Missouri to remain in the Union at the start of the Civil War.

Lyons was killed during a Civil War battle in 1861. In his will he bequeathed all of his estate to the federal government. (J.D., G.)

McALMOND CANYON. Named for Captain C.G. McAlmond of Potrero region, who was a sea officer for 18 years. In 1873 he became pilot commissioner for the port of San Diego. (J.D.) (See also under POTRERO.)

McCAIN VALLEY. A site in Carrizo district that was named for early homesteader John McCain, who settled here in 1869. He was especially noted as "one of the last of the old-fashioned cowboys."

McGINTY MOUNTAIN. Mrs. R. Dougherty has resided in El Cajon district for many years. She recalled that this nearby elevation was named after a mine owner here in the early 1900s, whose mine produced an element used for hardening ceramic products. He was known to have shipped his mineral throughout the U.S. and to Great Britain.

McGONIGLE CANYON. Named for Felix McGonigle, an early settler who homesteaded in Del Mar area. (Hu.) *The San Diego Union,* January 31, 1874, reported:

> Mr. Felix McGonigle of Soledad who has been laid up for sometime by a severe kick of a mule is out again, and was in town yesterday. We are glad to note his recovery.

MANGALAR SPRING. Long-time resident Mrs. A. Bergman of Aguanga recalled that "mangalar" was a Mexican name for the abundant sumac-type bushes that surrounded this spring in Yucca Valley.

MANZANITA INDIAN RESERVATION. (Spanish for "little apple.") Located in the Laguna Mountains. Its area is described as remote, with a few pockets of fertile valley land amidst barren rocks. (J.D.)

The San Diego Union, January 23, 1972, reported 7 residents on a land area of 3,579 acres on this reservation.

Indian dietary note: Manzanita fruit was gathered by the Indians when these berries turned yellow. After crushing the berries, they added water to make a refreshing drink.

MARGARITA PEAK. (See under SANTA MARGARITA.)

MARION CANYON. Named for the Marion family who homesteaded in the Pala district. The family's identity remains unknown.

MASON VALLEY. Designated for James E. Mason who homesteaded in Cuyamaca area in 1884. He was very familiar with the district, for he "carried the chain" for surveyors in the railroad survey of 1852. Until recently this district contained much artifact evidence that indicated earlier extensive Indian activity. (B.)

MATAGUAL CREEK. Probably a misspelling of *Mataquay,* an Indian name meaning "white earth," a reference to the white foam or lather that the Indians used as body paint. (Hu.) (Mesa Grande area.)

MERRIAM MOUNTAINS. Named for Major Gustavus F. Merriam who settled in San Marcos district in 1875, moving to this area for the sake of his wife's poor health. He owned 600 beehives and operated a successful winery. For many years he charted the rainfall for the federal weather bureau. The major was a descendant of Charles and George Merriam, publishers of Webster's dictionary. (J.D.)

Merriam's fearless and steadfast character soon won the admiration of the district. Cave Couts Senior declared the major to be a squatter on Couts's property, and he demanded — and later threatened — that Merriam vacate his new homestead — or else. Apparently possessing a temperament that Actor John Wayne could emulate, Merriam rejected and ignored the threats of Cave Couts and his armed vaqueros. Time — and resolute courage — established Merriam's legal possession of his homestead. (P. Rush, p. 23)

MESA GRANDE: Community, Indian Reservation. (Spanish for "large tableland.") It had been place-named "Mesaville" (a hybrid form), but residents preferred and petitioned successfully to change it to the original "Mesa Grande." The Indians called this area "Took-uh-mack," signifying "the place behind the ridge." (Hu.)

An attractive description of this community in 1885 was recorded in Van Dyke's *City and County of San Diego:*

> This tract is called Mesa Grande and contains some six thousand acres of splendid plow land. Here too you find plenty of springs and running brooks. The farms are still more like eastern farms than those of Ballena, a scarcity of rain is unknown, all crops and fruits are a certainty, and the farmers have no anxiety except the fear of too much rain. The whole area now looks like an eastern country with no resemblance whatever to the land thirty miles west, and three thousand feet below, the country from which all impressions of San Diego County are taken. (p. 36)

79

Mesa Grande Reservation is located below Lake Henshaw and west from Santa Ysabel Reservation. It is an attractive district of oak groves and mountains. The land was acquired by the Indians through an executive order in 1883. *The San Diego Union,* January 23, 1972, reported 38 residents on an area of 120 acres on this reservation.

Historical note: A news story in *The San Diego Union* of July 13, 1886, reported the discovery in Mesa Grande district of very rich gold quartz:

> ...which has put the whole camp in a fever of excitement. The quartz is described as fairly glittering with gold. The country in the vicinity is alive with prospectors.

METATE HILL. An apt descriptive appellation for an old Indian site in Anza-Borrego Desert where apparently were found numerous stones once used by Indians for pounding grain. Ranger Jack Welch named this ancient feature.

MEXICAN CANYON. Possibly a folk-name reference to a resident − or an incident that involved a Mexican national. This place in Jamul area was sometimes referred to as "Horsethief Canyon." (Hu.)

MIDDLE MESA PEAK. Cuyamaca Mountains consist of several peaks and ridges. Middle Mesa Peak lies between Cuyamaca Peak and North Peak. Its Indian name was "Igual," signifying "the broadest peak." The Mexicans in the area referred to this peak as "Las Nalgas" (the rump). (B.) (See also under CUYAMACA.)

MILDRED FALLS. According to *The San Diego Union,* May 7, 1973, the naming of this small waterfall in Ritchie Creek remains without verification. One old-time resident stated that an Indian girl named Mildred made a leaping suicide here; but another old-timer insisted that the falls were named for a childhood chum, Mildred Williams, who was a frequent visitor to this site. (Julian Creek.)

MILLER CREEK. An apparent personal name that remains unexplained.

MINERAL HILL. Was this place-name an indication of success — or disappointment — to prospectors? Its name origin is unknown. (Located in Cleveland National Forest.)

MINE WASH. This wash is located in an earlier mining area in Pinyon Mountains, hence its apparent descriptive name.

MIRAMAR. (Spanish for "sea view.") Place-named by Edward W. Scripps, newspaper publisher, in 1892. Scripps purchased 400 acres for $5,000. From a hilltop Scripps could see the ocean, and this view gave him the idea for its name. He was delighted with the location, for, he stated, "It's three thousand miles from the human beings connected with my newspapers." He also declared that the area reminded him of the coast of Algiers which once was his favorite vacation area.

"Miramar" is also the name of an attractive site on the island of Majorca where Father Junipero Serra was born. (J.D., B.)

MISSION: Bay, Valley. On the Portola expedition of 1769 Father Crespi referred to this bay as a "closed port" of San Diego Harbor. Father Font referred to the bay as "overflowed bay" *(Puerto Anegado)* during the 1774 expedition of Anza. It was later referred to as "False Bay" until the U.S. Geographic Board officially changed this place-name to Mission Bay in 1915.

Mission Valley was the early route of travel from the San Diego Presidio to the valley mission 6 miles east, established in 1774. (J.D., G.)

MOLLUSK WASH. Such a descriptive name records the earlier discovery of marine fossils in this dry stream bed. (Borrego Desert.)

MONKEY HILL. Tradition has it that padres from the *asistencia* in San Jose Valley often climbed to the top of this butte to pray, thereby folk-naming it "Monk's Hill." Over the years this name became corrupted into "Monkey Hill." (Lake Henshaw district.)

For a long time local tradition insisted that treasure was buried somewhere on the hill. (J.D.)

MONSERATE MOUNTAIN. (Spanish for "serrated ridge.") It is believed that an early Spanish homesteader fancied a resemblance between this California saw-toothed ridge in Pala region and that of the region of Monserrat Monastery near Barcelona, Spain. (J.D.)

Monserate Rancho was the outgrowth of a land grant by Governor Pio Pico in 1846 to Ysidro Maria Alvarado. Señor Alvarado was described as a kind of non-conformist by Judge Benjamin Hayes *(Pioneer Notes)* when the judge wrote somewhat plaintively:

> In the summer of 1858 I was at Don Ysidro's. . . .I do not know why Don Ysidro has not prospered more at Montserate. He seems to have few cattle, nor has there been much ground in cultivation; lives almost in Indian style. A clever tender-hearted man, like the rest of his name whom I have known. (p. 222)

MONUMENT PEAK. This is a frequent place-name for sites where surveyors have erected a "monument" of identified location. This peak, adjacent to Mt. Laguna, is almost 6300 feet high, and its monument is a heap of boulders five feet tall. The monument provided a check-point for the surveyors as they mapped the surrounding district. (J.D.)

MOONLIGHT CANYON. The source of this pleasant place-name image in Borrego Desert may have been the preference of a romantic pioneer or a sentimental surveyor.

MORENA: Village, Butte, Valley. A sentient place-name in San Diego County borrowed from Helen Hunt Jackson's *Ramona,* wherein the secondary character was Felipe Morena. (J.D.)

Historical suburban note: In 1887 a group of land developers incorporated the site of "Morena" on the eastern shore of False Bay. Their 1000 acres were to "afford attractive sites for suburban homes." Today's Morena Boulevard is the lone reminder of this "boom" suburb of 1887. (W. Smythe, p. 711)

Early San Diego festival memo:
Once more the Plaza is ornamented with an Oriental pavilion which has arisen at the call of the ladies of San Diego as a temporary bazaar where they may dispose of fruits and flowers, donated by different liberal individuals, in aid of the cause of benevolence. The scene within the tent is beautiful. The cooling fountain together with the ravishing perfumes of flowers and ripe fruits and sweet music from a professional band entices the visitor into forgetting that life is real. *(San Diego Advertiser,* August 20, 1891.)

MORENO VALLEY. This may be a misspelling of "Morena." (Lakeside area.)

MORGAN HILL. A personal place-name in Palomar district for Preacher Morgan, whose favorite Sabbath sermon was on "Temperance." Before the Morgan family settled here, the hill was believed to have provided a hideout for horse thieves. The hill has since been included in the Indian grazing lands of the district. (C. Wood, p. 66)

MORRO HILL. (Spanish for a "crown-shaped rock or hill.") The Luiseño Indians of San Luis Rey district regarded this isolated height as "a hill of the First People"; they had an interesting legend about this hill having been a refuge for their First People during a flood. (Hu.)

It also was referred to occasionally as "Sleeping Indian

Hill," from an Indian account that one of their maidens had died here and had been buried in a cave on the hill (according to Ernest Taylor, local Oceanside historian).

Historical note: It is probable that the Luiseño Indians preserved more star names than any other tribe in the county since they believed that dead persons were reincarnated as stars. For them the Milky Way was a representation of relationship with the spirits of those who had died. (L. Swain, p. 23)

MORTERO PALMS. (Spanish for "Indian mortars.") A descriptive place-name for the numerous bedrock mortars that are artifacts of the earlier Indians in Borrego Desert. (H. Parker, p. 79)

MOTHER GRUNDY PEAK. According to local history this peak in Dulzura district originally was designated as "Madre Grande" because it suggested the face of an older woman. Someone once jokingly said, "Madre Grande looks more like Mother Grundy to me," thereby inventing a new folk-form of name for the peak. (D. Schmid, p. 3)

MOTHER MIGUEL MOUNTAIN. The origin of this place-name in Sweetwater district remains unexplained.

MOUNTAIN PALM SPRINGS. A descriptive place-name for several small palm groves in the Carrizo district. These palm trees were an important resource that provided food and fiber for the desert Indians. As the redwood tree is a feature of Northern California, so also is the palm tree characteristic of the Southern California desert. (H. Parker, pp. 89-90)

MOUNT ARARAT. This borrowed or transferred biblical place-name was reported to have been bestowed by Ike Frazee, an early settler in the San Luis Rey district. A pioneer public notice of January 5, 1884, declared:

Elder Frazee will preach every second and fourth Lordsdays

at 11 o'clock a.m., and at lamplighting, at the same place. All are invited to attend. - - - James Griffin. (J.D.)

Apparently Ararat was a symbol of hope for Ike Frazee and his family as new settlers here – and likewise it might have been for other Mount Ararats place-named in Eldorado, Merced, and Plumas counties of California. (G.)

MOUNT GOWER. Santa Ysabel Postmaster Jeff Swycaffer recalled that this elevation in Ramona was referred to as "Black Horse Canyon" because of the presence of a wild, black stallion on this hill. However, it was later place-named "Gower" after an early surveyor in the district. (See also under BLACK MOUNTAIN.)

MOUNT LAGUNA. (See under LAGUNA.)

MOUNT OLYMPUS. Such a classical name-designation certainly suggests a lofty ideal for a not-so-lofty elevation. Alas, its name origin is unknown. (Located east from Rainbow.)

MOUNT TULE. Located in In-Ko-Pah district. (See under LOS TULES.)

MOUNT WHITNEY. William J. Whitney was a battle-scarred Civil War veteran who homesteaded near the top of this elevation in 1869 (San Marcos region), naming his homestead "Eden Vale." Living in hermit style and rarely encouraging visitors, he was regarded as an eccentric. (F. and L. Ryan, p. 170)

MULE HILL. A folk-form of name at a location in San Pasqual Valley. In 1846 starving American troops under General Kearny were besieged on this hill by a Spanish force under General Andres Pico. The shortage of food made it necessary for the American soldiers to use some of their mules for food. Hence the place-name. At times it has also been called "Starvation Hill" and "Battle Mountain." (J.D.)

MURPHY CANYON. A personal place-name for pioneer John Murphy, an Irish immigrant who settled here in 1860. The census of 1860 records his occupation as "teamster." As a homesteader Murphy cultivated almond and orange trees. His progress as a farmer was recorded in a *San Diego Union* classified ad (May 20, 1875):

> FOR SALE: The subscriber offers for sale his ranch in Mission Valley, known as Murphy Canyon, containing 260 acres, together with the improvements thereon, among which are 150 orange and almond trees. 60 acres of the ranch are well fenced. A splendid well of water is on the premises, with windmill, etc., complete. Price $2000. John Murphy.

Early county maps show Murphy Canyon, indicating its canyon road as a short cut into Poway Valley. (J.D., W.D.)

Historical nut tree memo: The first almond trees were planted in San Diego Mission gardens by the padres. Not until 1870 did some county farmers realize that almonds had a substantial market value. By 1900 their cultivation increased greatly throughout the county.

MURRAY: Reservoir, Canyon. James A. Murray was chiefly responsible for the construction of Murray Dam in 1916 in Mission Valley district. Murray had made a large fortune in mining in Montana before coming to San Diego. Gossipers whispered that he frequently carried $1000 in his coat pocket, and that he often had unset pearls and diamonds in his hip pocket.

The canyon was named for pioneer John Murray who homesteaded here with his family in the 1880s in Mission Valley area. (J.D., W.D.)

MUTH VALLEY. A personal place-name for A.M. Muth, a prominent beekeeper in the El Cajon and Alpine districts. (J.D.)

NATE HARRISON GRADE. A personal place-name for a black man by the name of Nate Harrison. He was regarded as a lovable character in the Palomar district. First brought to California as a slave, he made his way here after his master died in the northern gold region. At Palomar he became a sheepherder, lived with Indians for a while, and finally married an Indian woman with several children. The last of his years were spent homesteading a small ranch. After his death, funds were raised for a bronze plate and monument to be set at a turn of this grade which read:

> Nathan Harrison's Spring
> Brought here a slave about 1848
> Died October 10, 1920
> Aged 101 years
> 'A man's a man for a' that.'

(C. Wood, pp. 39-42)

NATIONAL CITY. In 1868 Warren and Frank Kimball bought 27,000 acres of land here and eventually built a modern city — a project actually competing with Alonzo Horton's "New San Diego." (Ha.)

In 1789 this land was a grazing area used by the San Diego Mission and was referred to as "La Purisima Concepcion." By 1795 it was known as "Rancho del Rey": a royal farm for the pasturage of horses and cattle of the presidio. With the advent of Mexican control, Rancho del Rey was renamed "El Rancho de la Nacion" (the national ranch). The Kimball brothers preserved that name in "National City." (J.D.)

The energy and foresight of the Kimball brothers made the present city a possibility. Without hesitation they subdivided the land, built a wharf, and encouraged agricultural experimentation — even a silk worm venture in 1870 which failed. By 1900 National City ranked second in population in the county.

Historical Civic Note: The wife of Warren Kimball was deeply interested in civic affairs. Clarence A. McGrew in *City of San Diego and San Diego County* reported:

> Mrs. Warren Kimball wrote many articles descriptive of Southern California and of the San Diego Bay region. Her articles on woman suffrage attracted much attention. She was the first woman elected to the school board of National City and also was active in the establishment of the city's free public library. (p. 382)

The first San Diego County Fair occurred in National City, opening September 22, 1880, another promotion of progress by the Kimball brothers. It was called "Horticultural Fair of 1880." Two days after the Fair's opening *The San Diego Union* reported:

> People were not prepared to witness such a scene as awaited them: fruits, vegetables, embroidery work, hair and fern work, shell work, and different types of paintings. Ball games at the foot of 7th Avenue. Some of the finest horses in the state have been brought here for display. No racing.
>
> Visitors from Granges 700 miles away came to National City and had to wait their turn to see the displays. The New England Kitchen gave anyone a dinner such as they never dreamed of for 25 cents, and the Fair closed with a dance.

Today's National Avenue in this city was the first road the Kimballs ordered built. In 1974 the population of National City ranked seventh in the county.

NELSON CANYON. Named for an early pioneer in Descanso district whose identity is unknown.

NESTOR. San Diego community near Imperial Beach, place-named for Nestor A. Young, popular state assemblyman 1884-1886. He was appointed harbormaster for San Diego in 1889. (J.D.)

Biographical memo: the following classified ad appeared in *The San Diego County Advertiser,* August 6, 1891:

> IDEAL FARM FOR SALE. 279 acres, 47 miles from San Diego, 24 miles from R.R. terminus, ½ mile from store and P.O. same to first grade school ten months of the year. 100 acre A1 corn, vegetable, or alfalfa land, will grow any fruit, cereal, or vegetable indigenous to the climate without irrigation; 12 living springs providing running water year round; rare chance for fish ponds; 15 acres fenced into 8 sub-divisions with 3 to 8 wires and posts 9 feet apart; 4 acres fine bearing orchard 5 to 12 years old; 4 acres fine bearing apples, cherries, pears, peaches, plums, apricots, nectarines, figs, quinces and almonds, also strawberries, gooseberries, currants, and one acre of heavy bearing blackberries. House of 8 rooms, chicken house, sheds, etc. Plenty of timber for all time. This is a farm in every sense of the word and any practical farmer who will attend to business can make $1,500 annually on this place. Price of farm including farming utensils, span of horses and wagon, 2 cows, 8 hogs, and 3 dozen chickens, $9,000. Terms ½ cash, balance on time. Call on or address Nestor A. Young, San Diego, California.
>
> P.S. Domestic troubles alone are the cause of placing this farm on the market. Hence no offers of exchange for other properties would be entertained.

NOBLE CANYON. Named for brothers Jack and Tom Noble who operated a successful gold mine in Pine Valley district. Jack was remembered as a man who always had a pistol at his hip, and who was an unusual marksman with the weapon. Jack died in 1932. Several years later brother Tom scrapped the mine machinery and beneath it he found $1100 worth of ore. (Bob Lee, *Lost Mines and Buried Treasures of San Diego County,* pp. 13-14)

NOLINA WASH. A descriptive place-name for a yucca-type plant not common to Anza-Borrego district. The plant grows on the slopes of this wash. (J.S. Chase, p. 375)

NORTH ISLAND. Mrs. Charles Mackenzie, founder of the Coronado Historical Association, recalled her childhood play at a narrow strand of beach that was flooded for several hours daily by high tide. Parents forbade their children to play here, she reported, warning them of quicksand danger. The high tide caused a daily separation of "north" and "south" island. Navy control included a plan to fill in this low strand, thereby eliminating its ebb and flow. Local usage of "south island" disappeared.

The earliest known name for this peninsula was "La Ysla" (the island). It was later land-granted in 1846 by Governor Pico to Don Pedro C. Carillo as "Peninsula de San Diego Rancho." The grant comprised 4,000 acres, described as ample for at least two cattle sites. (W.D. See also under CORONADO.)

NORTH PEAK. This is the northern peak of the group of Cuyamaca Mountains with an elevation over 6000 feet. Its Indian name was "Galcacuise" or "the bunch." (See also under CUYAMACA.) (B., J.D.)

NORTH PINYON MOUNTAINS. (See under PINYON.)

NORTH WASH. A descriptive name for a site near Agua Caliente Hot Springs.

NUDE WASH. The wash is located close to Highway 78 just east of the Narrows. Park Ranger Merle Beckman folk-named it after having observed a nude male strolling there one day.

OAK: Grove, Canyon, Spring. Oak Grove, northwest from Warner Springs, was on the Butterfield stage route to Temecula. It was an earlier travelers' stopover, mentioned occasionally in diaries and letters of passengers who used this trail into California. After enduring the inhospitable desert from Yuma, passing through dry and sandy canyons, weary travelers must have found Oak Grove a welcome overnight halt. During the Civil War the Union established a military post, Camp Wright, near Oak Grove — to prevent California secessionists from reaching Confederate forces in Arizona, and to be a staging station for Union troops to march on Fort Yuma, Arizona. (J.D.)

OAKZANITA PEAK. This is an unusual hybrid or coined place-name *(oak* plus *manzanita)* to designate the abundance of oak and manzanita growth in Cuyamaca State Park district. (J.D.)

The manzanita shrub can be found all over California, varying from a "creeper" to a tall-growing shrub. Gudde reports more than 100 geographic features place-named for this unusual wild plant.

OAT HILLS. A descriptive place-name in Escondido district where wild oat fields once were abundant.

OCEANA. This appears to be a coined name for an earlier suburb adjacent to Oceanside.

OCEANSIDE. According to local tradition this was a place "that just named itself": before 1884 it had been the custom for families "to go oceanside" here, their favorite location for beach outings. Local history reported that Mrs. Jack Meyer insisted on the name "Oceanside" for this settlement. (James Hyne)

Jack Meyer was the first owner of a house at this site. But Chauncey Hayes was inspired in 1886 to promote Oceanside as a "boom" enterprise. Very soon a small city flourished where a barren mesa had previously existed, and Oceanside had already been place-named before it became a settlement. (J.D., Ha.)

Oceanside became one of the most successful boom towns of "ocean and climate" fame on the southern California coast. A newspaper item in 1887 predicted it was "destined to be the Cape May and Long Branch of the Coast." (G. Dumke, p. 149)

In 1974 Oceanside ranked fourth in population in the county.

1894 Back County Hustle-Bustle:

Oceanside street improvement is progressing. Vacant lots in the heart of town are being sowed with grain. *(San Diego County Advertiser,* January 27, 1894.)

OCOTILLO: Badlands, Flat, Wells. (Spanish for "thorny.") A descriptive place-name after the abundance of the ocotillo shrub in the Anza-Borrego Desert. It is a desert plant with cactaceous habits, but it is not a species of cactus. Its brilliant, red flower has generated nicknames of "desert candlewood," "flaming sword," "coach whip," and "fire poker."

The ocotillo flower was a regular part of desert-Indian nutrition. Desert ranchers used the thicker ocotillo branches as fencing material around gardens and homes. (J.S. Chase, p. 369)

OLIVENHAIN. (German for "home of the olive.") This was a colony project by a group of German-Americans from the eastern U.S. Their organizational prospectus of 1884 declared agriculture as their proposed principal occupation. Further, their German-language prospectus declared "necessary capital is $200, $25 entry fee into the group, $100 down payment on real estate, and $75 for about three months' living expense." It also reported that olive trees flourished in the district, and that the organizers were certain that their olive colony could be guaranteed a prosperous and good life.

The lack of sufficient water and a rocky soil soon doomed the hopes and aspirations of the 69 families in the colony. *(San Diego Union,* July 17, 1966.)

This place-name originally was spelled "Olivenheim." (J.D.)

Historic agriculture note: Olive oil was an essential ingredient of Spanish and Mexican food preparation. The olive tree in California supplied a basic dietary need wherever a mission was founded, and the first olive trees were cultivated at San Diego Mission. Soon olive trees were growing up and down the coast.

The designation "Mission Olive" is today's fossil of a San Diego "first." In the twentieth century, however, the importance of the olive succumbed to progress. Example: In recent years an extensive county olive grove was transformed into Singing Hills Golf Course in El Cajon district.

OLLA WASH. This Borrego Desert hybrid place-name probably is a descriptive designation for *ollas*, Indian-type pots, found here — or even perhaps a special site for making ollas?

O'NEAL CANYON. Long-time resident Mrs. Claudell Kuebler recalled that this was the name of an early homesteader in Otay area. Although Mr. O'Neal eventually moved out of the county, this name for the canyon was retained by later surveyors.

O'NEILL LAKE. Named for Richard O'Neill who at one time owned Santa Margarita Ranch. (B., J.D.)

ONOFRE HILL. (See under SAN ONOFRE.)

OPATA CREEK. This apparent personal place-name in Miramar area remains unexplained.

ORIFLAMME: Canyon, Mountains. (French for "gold flame.") These are geographical places named for the famous Oriflamme gold mine of 1870 in the Julian district. No direct information is available concerning the designation of this place-name. However, a sidewheel steamship named "Oriflamme" made scheduled calls at San Diego Harbor as part of its passage from San Francisco to the Atlantic Ocean. One might conjecture a connection between the Oriflamme steamer and the Oriflamme mine because of their "gold" prefixes. (J.D.)

Historical travel memo: *San Diego County Advertiser,* August 13, 1891, routinely reported:

Travel between San Diego and Los Angeles is large these days and preference is marked for the trip by steamer. The Pacific Coast Steamship officials are courteous and obliging; and on the ocean highway there is neither dust nor flies but solid comfort, all of which the passenger duly appreciates.

OROSCO RIDGE. The identity of this personal place-name in Ramona district is uncertain. It may have been designated for Jose Maria Orozco (sic) who received the land grant for Rancho Guejito in 1845.

OTAY: Settlement, Mesa, Mountain, River, Valley. The translation of this Indian name varies: either "wide and level place" or "brushy place."

Otay was the site of an earlier Indian *rancheria* (village). In 1846 Rancho Otay was land-granted to Magdalena Estudillo, member of a prominent family in early San Diego history. In 1887 the "boom" town of Otay was promoted by real estate developers Guion, Hartley, and Hamilton. The place-name of Otay was retained from the rancho name.

Jose Estudillo, brother of Magdalena, is remembered in San Diego history as the owner of Casada Estudillo which years later attained historical significance as "Ramona's Marriage Place" in Old Town.

In 1883 John Joseph Montgomery made a brief glider flight at Otay Mesa. (P. Rush, pp. 8 - 9)

PALA: Creek, Indian Reservation, Mission, Mountain. (Indian for "place of water.") These place-names derive from an early Indian village of the same name. It is believed that Pala was a gathering-place for large numbers of Indians long before the Spanish arrival in 1769. With the establishment of San Luis Rey Mission, this area became an extremely fertile rancho of the Mission, developing as a home and labor center for more than 1000 Indians. (J.D., G.)

In 1903 the Indians at Warner Springs were dispossessed, and Pala was selected as their new home. Here they settled, with great bitterness at first, to become farmers in a most fertile and scenic district. According to *The San Diego Union* of January 22, 1972, 255 Indians resided here on 1700 acres at that date.

Helen Hunt Jackson reported her inspection visit to Pala Reservation in her *Century of Dishonor*.

PALM: Canyon, City, Mesa, Spring. The largest of true desert trees is the fan palm which often grows eighty feet tall. To the passing desert traveler the sight of the palm tree suggested a place of water and shade. For the desert Indians the palm tree provided food, and materials of functional utility. These palms are not date trees (which the early Spanish brought). They were here a long time before humans. And their uniqueness and singular presence have suggested various place-names in both San Diego and Riverside counties. Palm Canyon, Spring, and Mesa are located in Anza-Borrego Desert.

Palm City was established in 1914. Its original place-name was "Palm Avenue" after the attractive avenue of planted palms on its main artery. The Post Office objected to this name, protesting that it could be a confusing form of mail address. Thereupon it became Palm City. (Hu.)

PALOMAR MOUNTAIN. (Spanish for "place of the pigeon.") This descriptive place-name was part of a Mexican land grant of 1846, Cañada de Palomar. Its Indian name was *Paauw* or "mountain." When the Spanish came up the mountain to cut timber for use at the San Luis Rey Mission, they were impressed by the sight and cooing of pigeon flocks. Accordingly, they named the site "Palomar." In 1868 a homesteader, Joseph Smith, was found murdered on his ranch. Smith evidently had been popular in the district, for the mountain was renamed Smith Mountain in his memory.

However, the name "Palomar" was officially reestablished in 1901 by the U.S. Geographic Board, in response to a petition by local citizens for such a name-change. (J.D., Ha.)

Paauw was the Indians' summer mountain campsite, having a great abundance of berries, seeds, acorns, deer, and bulbs. And during the 1890s Palomar was a popular summer resort — with three hotels and a small tent camp in Doane Valley. (C. Wood, p. 13)

PALO VERDE: Canyon, Lake, Spring, Wash. The Spanish word "palo" can mean a log, timber, or mast; however, in California it was used to designate a tree. In the desert "palo verde" signified a tree with a smooth, green bark. Hence the descriptive place-name. (G.)

This singular desert tree produces scanty, short-lived foliage and often extends to a height of 30 feet. (J.S. Chase, p. 369)

The canyon and spring are near Borrego Springs; the lake is in Alpine district; and the wash lies east from Fonts Point in the desert.

PAMO VALLEY. A Pamo Indian village is mentioned in Spanish records in 1778. "Pamo" is a Diegueño word of unknown meaning. (G.)

PANAWATT SPRING. An apparent Indian name that remains unexplained. (Anza-Borrego Desert.)

PARADISE MOUNTAIN. A local historian, Abel Davis, reported that in 1864 two prospectors were panning for gold in Rincon Canyon on an unusually hot, sultry day. Bad luck and solar absorption soon discouraged and discomforted them. Climbing up the mountainside to its peak, they were refreshed by a cool breeze and a nearby cold spring. One sourdough declared, "This is the beginning of Paradise." This remark of relief and comfort thus designated the mountain's place-name. (Abel Davis, *Memoirs of Abel Davis,* p. 3)

Erwin Gudde reports more than 50 "Paradise" name-places in California.

PAUMA: Valley, Indian Reservation. The Indian meaning of this name may have been "place of little water." This was the place-name of an Indian village when it was visited in 1795 by Sergeant Grijalva and Padre Juan Mariner. Theirs was the first recorded San Diego group to explore the adjacent mountains. They named the district "Santa Maria." From here they explored south, naming Santa Ysabel and San Jose (Warner Springs) districts.

In 1833 a Mexican land grant established Santa Maria Rancho. The city of Ramona is located in this former Pauma and rancho district. (P. Rush, pp. 75-79)

According to *The San Diego Union* of January 23, 1972, the Pauma Reservation of 250 acres had 59 Indian residents at that date.

PECHSTEIN RESERVOIR. William Pechstein was an early land developer in Vista district and prominent in the early attempts to establish an irrigation scheme for this area.

PENA SPRING. This apparent personal place-name remains unexplained. (Anza-Borrego Desert.)

PEÑASQUITAS. (See under LOS PEÑASQUITOS.)

PENINSULA DE SAN DIEGO RANCHO. This jog-trot-sounding place-name was a land grant in 1846 by Governor Pio Pico to Don Pedro Carrillo, a member of a prominent Californio family of which movie actor Leo Carillo was a descendant.

Following the Mexican occupation, the rancho was a seesaw of legal contention by several claimants before the U.S. Land Commission in 1858. (R.W. Brackett, pp. 58-59) (See also under NORTH ISLAND and CORONADO.)

PETERSON CANYON. The identity of this apparent personal place-name in Alpine district is unknown.

PEUTZ VALLEY. Nicholas Peutz, a German immigrant, settled in Alpine district in the 1870s. He was known to make excellent charcoal (from live oak wood) which was used commercially to smoke meats.

PILGRIM CREEK. Charles Pilgrim farmed in Oceanside district in the 1880s. He was reported to have been a horse breeder and a grain and lima bean farmer.

PINE VALLEY. This area was known as "El Valle de los Piños" until Captain William S. Emery homesteaded here in 1869, anglicizing its place-name to Pine Valley. Emery learned of this area's availability from an Indian acquaintance, and the two men explored the area. Finding an Indian camping here, Emery offered to purchase the site. The native owner was willing, asking for a horse so that he could leave the area comfortably. Emery supplied the seller with a horse and saddle. When moving his family to Pine Valley in a covered wagon drawn by six mules, the Captain had to travel by way of Tijuana, Tecate, and Campo, for there was no road from San Diego to Pine Valley. The trip required four days.

From 1869 to 1874 Captain Emery operated a stage station line that carried passengers and mail from Los Angeles and San Diego into the desert. The Emery family were among the most prominent pioneers in county history. (J.D.)

PINYON: Mountain, Peak, Canyon, Wash. (From the Spanish *piñon* for "pine tree.") This place-name denotes the popular recognition of abundant pine growth throughout California. These mountains in Anza-Borrego Desert provided pine nuts for the Indians – and frequent disappointment for Yankee prospectors. However, some of its canyons and lower slopes furnished water and pasturage for desert stockmen. (See under HARPER CANYON.)

POGGI CANYON. A personal place-name for Joseph Poggi, an Italian immigrant, who became a cattleman in Otay district.

POSER MOUNTAIN. Located north from Descanso, this was designated for Heinrich von Poser, an early settler in the district. In 1873 he was inspector of elections for his area. Poser was listed on the military rolls for 1881.

Urban note: Up until 1913 there were four old streetcars used as summer cottages at the summit of Poser Mountain (elevation 3917 feet). No one – not even the streetcar company – could determine how these cars arrived where they were. (See Vertical File P-W, San Diego Historical Society, Serra Museum Library.)

POTRERO: Settlement, Peak, Creek. (Spanish for "meadow or pasturing place.") This site was first settled in 1868 by sea captain Charles McAlmond, a native of Maine. His family were the first non-Indians to homestead here, just a short distance from the Mexican border. (J.D.)

Ella McCain, who lived in the south section of the county for 85 years, sketched a vignette of early Potrero in the following memoir:

> From signs left in the rocks, Potrero Valley must have been inhabited for many, many years by Indians but when the first white settlers came to the valley, they had gone away or had been driven farther back into the mountains by the Mexicans or other Indian tribes which they were often in trouble with. I have been told Potrero is a Spanish word and means 'pasture'; and rightly so, for I will never forget my first glimpse of the valley. It was beautiful with its hundreds of large oaks, elders, and sycamores. For years the early settlers hired Indians and Mexicans to cut the trees into cordwood, the teamsters hauled freight for this back country, bought the wood and sold it in San Diego for fuel. The bark was used for tanning leather and smoking meat; a tea was made from oak bark and blackberry root which was used extensively in the treatment for bad cases of diarrhea. Ink was very scarce in those days and some of the settlers made their own ink from the juice of green oak balls of the bush oaks. They squeezed the juice into bottles and dropped in a few rusty nails or a bit of rusty iron, and soon had very good ink. (Ella McCain, *Memories of the Early Settlements, Dulzura, Potrero, and Campo*, p. 54)

Potrero Creek is located in the Pauma Valley region.

POWAY: Settlement, Valley. (Indian for "place where the valley ends.") This site is mentioned in 1828 as a rancho of Mission San Diego ("Paguay"). It is also shown on a *diseño* (plat) of Rancho San Bernardo as "Cañada y Arroyo de Paguay." It was first homesteaded in 1858 by Philip Crosthwaite, who used the valley as a cattle range. (G., J.D.)

The San Diego Union, January 1, 1894, reported a shift in use of land:

> ...for a considerable period of time, this region was exclusively occupied by stockmen. Then under the new order, grain growing was introduced. About 1873 Dr. French and S.G. Blaisdell commenced planting fruit trees and vines. The results proved so favorable that they gradually enlarged their operations and others were led to follow their example.

In 1892 the community was reported to have the school district with the most money in its treasury. Also in 1892 Poway was declared a temperance community, and no saloon was permitted within its boundaries. *(The San Diego Union,* August 1, 1892.)

POWDER DUMP WASH. When Highway 78 was built through the Narrows, the crew established a dynamite storage vault in this wash. Park Ranger Clyde Strickler named it. (Ranger Jack Welch)

PROCTOR VALLEY. A personal place-name designated for an eminent English astronomer, Professor Richard Proctor. In 1887 his widow arrived in National City with a plan to establish an observatory atop San Miguel Mountain as a memorial to her husband. Apparently much discourse and negotiation proceeded over several years. The memorial plan eventually was abandoned by Mrs. Proctor, as the community would not provide the cash for her project. Meanwhile, during the years of 1887-1892 the valley had been often referred to as Proctor Valley, and thereby a commemoration — without formal ceremony — was applied by citizens of the district. (Herbert C. Hensley, *Memoirs of Herbert C. Hensley,* Vol. II.)

PUEBLITOS CANYON. (Spanish for "little pueblo.") In Spanish California, "pueblo" was a common generic name corresponding to the American "town." This canyon may have been named for an Indian pueblo of 1835 in Rancho Santa Margarita district.

PYGMY GROVE. A site in Sweeney Pass whose intriguing name is a mystery.

QUAIL CANYON. One of these descriptive place-names for this wild bird is in Santee district, and another Quail Canyon is in San Pasqual district. Erwin Gudde reports 25 geographic quail name-places, indicating the abundance of these birds in earlier California.

Historical note: One hundred years ago flocks of 1000 or more quail were common. Hunters shot great quantities of quail for commercial marketing. Their numbers, as a consequence, were greatly diminished.

The quail is the official California state bird. The selection of a state bird began in 1928 in the California state legislature. A bird was to be chosen whose plumage, song, and quality were unique to — yet typical of — the Golden State. Further: no bird was to be proposed if it already was a symbol for another state; the selected bird must be of no nuisance to farmers or of no harm to crops; and it must have food habits that would entitle it to protection under the law.

Later that year the formerly ubiquitous quail was declared winner of this California legislative competition. (N. Greene, *History of California*, Scrapbook I , pp. 6-8)

RAINBOW: Settlement, Spring, Wash. Peter Larsen was the first homesteader here in 1870. In 1888 J.P.M. Rainbow and a partner purchased land for a townsite which included Larsen's homestead. Mr. Rainbow proposed Larsen's name for the new settlement. Larsen countered with "Rainbow," stating that such a name had much more meaning than just a personal name — that it implied the fabled pot of gold. Thereby the town became so named. (J.D.)

In 1890 J.P.M. Rainbow was elected a San Diego County Supervisor. His residence and county service, however, were somewhat brief. Shortly afterward, Riverside County was carved out of San Diego County, and the new county lines divided Mr. Rainbow's property — the house was now in Riverside County and the barn in San Diego County! Thereupon Mr. Rainbow resigned as County Supervisor, contending that he had no intention of taking up residence in his barn. *(The Enterprise,* August 29, 1968, Fallbrook)

The origin of the names of Rainbow Spring and Rainbow Wash in other areas of the county remains unexplained. (Because of rainbow-colored stratified rock nearby? Or a vision of a rainbow?)

RAMONA. Place-named after the heroine of Helen Hunt Jackson's novel. The modern town of Ramona began when Bernard Etchenverry, a Basque sheep rancher, donated a piece of land to Amos Verlaque with the condition that he open a store. Verlaque promptly erected the settlement's store building. Soon other stores were built, and in 1883 the community was named "Nuevo" (new). In 1886 the Santa Maria Water and Land Company laid out the present site which included the earlier Nuevo. (J.D., W.D.)

The land company designated "Ramona" as its place-name. The Post Office in Washington rejected this name, stating another Ramona existed in Los Angeles County. This latter town, however, eventually became defunct, and the name was now a free agent.

The Santa Maria Land Company opportunely and officially discarded "Nuevo" in 1895 for the present "Ramona" (which is located on Rancho Santa Maria land grant of 1833).

Historical realty note: the squabble as to who was first with the place-name of Ramona was announced by a San Diego realty office in a most unorthodox real estate advertisement:

> Only a few years ago that interesting squaw (Ramona) was wandering up and down San Diego County, with never a corner lot she could call her own, and only the sheep-shearing, horse-nipping, sad-eyed son of the soil to wit: "Allesandro" for company. Now, under the inspiration of Helen Hunt Jackson's genius, every enterprising land-speculator who is lying in wait for the soft and sentimental side of a Boston tenderfoot, rushes to name a creek, a town, or a street as "Ramona." We do not complain of this, but we think that Los Angeles real estate sharps who are trying to carve sanitariums out of fog-banks ought to keep their predatory hands at home. . . .
>
> Ramona, the squaw, the creature of the gifted Helen Hunt Jackson's brain, has passed on with her creator 'over the ridge', but Ramona, the beautiful center of a beautiful valley, will live and grow and be the center of the most attractive home life in the state. *(The San Diego Union,* January 1, 1887.)

The Diegueño Indians called the locality ·"Mutarati," or "place of big valley." (J.D.)

RANCHITA. (Spanish for "small ranch.") Otto Fabian, settler at this site, applied for a post office station in 1935 under the name of "Ranchito." An apparent error in Washington printed this name as "Ranchita." Fabian was its first postmaster.

RANCHO SAN BERNARDO. This district of San Bernardo Rancho appears on maps as early as 1800. An Indian *rancheria* (village) called Rancho San Dieguito existed earlier here along the San Dieguito River. During the mission period this was a cattle ranch under the control of San Diego Mission. San Bernardo Rancho comprised over 17,000 acres as a land grant in 1842 to Captain Joseph Snook, who had become a naturalized Mexican in 1833.

It remained as a grazing range for thousands of Black Angus cattle until 1961 when a combine of Texas oil men purchased the land with plans to subdivide it. Where not so long ago jack rabbits gamboled and cattle grazed, now stands a flourishing settlement of twentieth-century progress. (P. Rush, pp. 43-45)

San (Saint) Bernardo was named after a theologian of the Middle Ages who was one of the leaders of the Second Crusade, and who drew up, in 1128, the statutes of the once famous Knights Templars.

RANCHO SANTA FE. (Spanish for "Holy Faith.") The history of this settlement has been described as a development "from sagebrush to sumac, to eucalyptus and citrus, to sophisticated residents and singular estates."

As early as 1778 the San Diego Mission declared jurisdiction over the Indian village which the Mission designated as San Dieguito Rancheria. In 1840 Juan Maria Osuna received a land grant of over 8,000 acres in this district. In 1906 the land was purchased by the Santa Fe railroad for $100,000. The railroad planned an experimental planting of eucalyptus trees to provide usable wood for railroad ties. Three million of these trees, imported from Australia and New Zealand, were set out. The scheme proved to be a failure when it soon became apparent that eucalyptus wood could not hold railroad spikes securely.

Soon after World War I California enjoyed another citrus boom period. And the Santa Fe Railroad by 1921 decided to capitalize on this growth. Vice-President W.E. Hodges (for whom Hodges Dam was named) became manager of a land development project, San Dieguito Rancho was renamed "Rancho Santa Fe," and by 1930 the land development was a success. Copying a proven British plan of protective building control, Santa Fe's contemporary residents accept a regulated administration of their community with a restriction of architectural, landscaping, and commercial standards in their community. ("Rancho Santa Fe," *Union Title Trust Topics,* 1948, pp. 2-7)

A strong Spanish architectural emphasis is a feature of Rancho Santa Fe — and this same Spanish accent is evident in the sophisticated names of its streets.

RATTLESNAKE: Canyon, Creek, Spring. An apt descriptive name-designation after these serpents in this Anza-Borrego Desert area. Erwin Gudde reports nearly 200 such geographical places in the state of California.

RED: Mountain, Top. This descriptive place-name was usually applied because of some geographical feature of red color. Next to black, red is a most repeated adjective of color for place-names in California — and throughout the U.S. (G.) The mountain is in Pala district, and Red Top is in Anza-Borrego Desert.

REIDY CANYON. Early homesteader Maurice Reidy was great-uncle to Frances Ryan, native and long-time resident of Escondido. In her interesting history, *Early Days In Escondido,* she vignettes her pioneering relatives:

"Here is our home!" Maurice Reidy's vow broke the monotony of creaking and plodding oxen. From the brow of the hill the weary family gazed at the vista of a peaceful little valley secluded in foothills. In 1850 Maurice had driven his ox team in a covered wagon caravan across the plains in the rush for California gold. His bride, Julia, followed him to Placer County and joined in the seeking. After a decade of mining, money gone and family growing, the disillusioned couple hitched the ox team and trekked southward hunting a spot to settle down. At first sight their hearts were set on a hidden valley home but Rancho Rincon del Diablo belonged to San Diego Judge Witherby. The nearest government land open to homesteaders was four miles north of the present Escondido city. The Reidys settled there and proved up on a patent to 160 acres of fertile land in 1869. One Jersey cow, which had trailed the wagon, was the nucleus of their prosperous dairy farm. Upon the death of Maurice Reidy Senior (1882), Maurice Reidy Jr. inherited the homestead. Today modern homes nestle among leafy grapevines in the area which bears their name "Reidy Canyon." (Frances and Lewis Ryan, *Early Days in Escondido,* p. 11)

Historical "buyers beware" memo: *The San Diego County Advertiser* editorially complained on August 27, 1891:

It appears from the action of some of our retail merchants that they, as well as their customers, are becoming tired of the unwarranted and wholly inexcusable custom of putting up butter in rolls weighing 1 3/4 pounds each and compelling the public to accept it and pay for it as 2 pounds. Why on earth 16 ounces avoirdupois should legally constitute a pound in Oregon and every other state in the Union, and only 14 ounces be obtainable for a pound in California is past our understanding. . . .Let every consumer boycott the notorious short weight rolls by purchasing only from packages in bulk, and it will not be long before the 14 ounce butter racket will be a thing of the past.

RICKEY LAKE. An apparent personal place-name in Sweetwater region whose identity remains unknown.

RINCON: Indian Reservation, Springs, del Diablo. (Spanish for "corner or angle.") The word signifies "the inside angle formed by the junction of two lines." Its Indian name was *Wasgha,* or "grass or reed." (G., W.D.)

"The Corners" would be an American designation for Rincon. (See also under ESCONDIDO.)

Rincon Reservation is located in Pauma district. In 1886 Helen Hunt Jackson described the reservation in *The Present Condition of Mission Indians in Southern California:*

> The Rincon is at the head of the valley, snuggled up against the mountains, as its name signifies, in a "corner." Here were fences, irrigating ditches, fields of barley, wheat, hay, and peas; a little herd of horses and cows grazing, and several flocks of sheep. The men were all away sheep-shearing; the women were at work in the fields, some hoeing, some clearing out the irrigating ditches and all the old women plaiting baskets. These Rincon Indians, we were told, had refused a school offered them by the government; they said they would accept nothing at the hands of the government until it gave them a title to their lands. (p. 527)

ROBLAR CREEK. (Spanish for "deciduous oak.") A descriptive place-name in Santa Margarita district.

ROCK HAVEN SPRING. Long-time Poway resident Mrs. Mary van Dam recollected the site of this spring that coursed large boulders. She remembered the existence of a small dwelling here at one time: a signboard on this hut was titled, "Rock Haven."

ROCKHOUSE CANYON. This descriptive place-name in Carrizo district in the desert is for a cattleman's shack built of stone and mortar. (H. Parker, p. 88)

ROCK MOUNTAIN. There are two of these descriptive features: one is in Otay Valley, and the other is in El Capitan Dam district.

ROCKWOOD CANYON. Named for B.B. Rockwood, an early settler in Pasqual Valley district. He was reported to have been the first in his district to plant a eucalyptus grove. *(Escondido Times Advocate,* Nov. 13, 1936.) (See also under RANCHO SANTA FE.)

Historical eucalyptus memo: The earliest date for a eucalyptus tree planted in the county was declared to be about 1800, although other first-planting claims were numerous and widespread.

The story of the eucalyptus tree "boom" in San Diego County history was drolly interpreted by Leland G. Stanford:

Not since pagan veneration of the sacred oaks of Jupiter have trees received the honor that three generations of San Diegans have bestowed upon the eucalyptus variety.

San Diegans planted olive trees by the hundreds, citrus trees by the thousands, and eucalyptus by the multi-million. Olive and citrus indeed contributed to bodily welfare, but the coming of the eucalyptus from Australia was, to many people, the long awaited Millenium – practically a supernatural beneficence to every area of life: economical, medicinal, and ethereal. Eucalyptus provided not only wonder wood and wonder drugs, but wonder miracles. Indeed, to many early Americans it was 'wunderbar'. . . .

For a number of years after the mid-nineteenth century it appeared that almost no part of southern California's business life would avoid revolutionary but beneficial changes from the introduction of the eucalyptus. Some of the big dreams became mere illusions; other phenomenal prospects failed to materialize only because San Diegans of the Victorian age, as fate willed it, were born thirty years too late (not too soon). "San Diego's Eucalyptus Bubble," *Journal of San Diego History,* Fall 1970, p. 11.

ROCKY PEAK. A descriptive geographic name-designation for a land feature northwest from De Luz.

RODRIGUEZ: Mountain, Canyon. Abe Rodriguez, long-time resident and farmer in Valley Center district, reported that "Rodriguez" was a frequent family name for Christianized Indians. He recalled that a family of that name lived in an Indian village named Cuca Rancho at the base of Rodriguez Mountain. He conjectured that the mountain was probably named for this family.

Rodriguez Canyon is located east from Lake Cuyamaca. Its name identity remains unexplained.

ROSE CANYON. Louis Rose was a prominent and industrious citizen of San Diego City. He arrived in San Diego in 1850 from Texas and soon became a most enterprising and highly regarded resident. Roseville, now known as part of Point Loma neighborhood, was his land development. Rose served as postmaster at Old Town for 10 years. He established a successful tannery in the canyon that is designated for him. (J.D.)

Portola's exploration party halted in this canyon on their way north. Cosmographer Costanso recorded this site in his diary, July 14, 1769:

> We halted in a canyon to which we gave the name of San Diego and where there was an abundance of pasture.

ROSECRANS: Fort, Avenue. Named for General William S. Rosecrans, considered an outstanding strategist in the Union Army. The general became Minister to Mexico in 1868 and later served as congressman from Los Angeles district, 1880-1884. (G.) As a private citizen he participated in various railroad and real estate promotions in San Diego.

Rosecrans Avenue is a street name in Los Angeles as well as in San Diego.

ROSS LAKE. A personal place-name whose identity is not known. (Located near De Luz.)

ROUND GRANITE HILL. This twin-named descriptive designation is a site in Borrego Desert. It is a common type of name throughout the U.S.

110

ROUND MOUNTAIN. This is a pristinely descriptive name-form for the shape of this land feature in Jacumba.

ROUND POTRERO. (Spanish for "meadow.") A dual language name-description of a circular pasture area or meadow at Barrett district.

RUSTY SPRING. The color of its water possibly suggested the name of this spring in Tubb Canyon.

SACATONE SPRING. (Spanish for "grass or hay.") Sacatone is a stiff bunch-grass usually found in alkaline soil. It often served as a desert forage for cattle and horses. (J.S. Chase, p. 369) (Located north from Boulevard.)

SALT CREEK. A repeated descriptive place-name applied throughout the world. San Diego County has two such creeks, in Otay and Cuyamaca areas.

SALVADOR CANYON. Place-named for the first baby born to a family of Anza's second expedition through the desert. (H. Parker, p. 28) (See also under THOUSAND PALMS.)

SAMAGATUMA VALLEY. An Indian name-designation whose meaning is not known. The Indian *rancheria* named "Samatayune" was recorded in Cuyamaca district about 1845. Its present name possibly is a corruption of the earlier name. (J.D.)

SAN CLEMENTE CANYON. An official report on the 1872 survey of ex-mission lands includes the following:

> ...about one league from the Mission building is the Cañada Clemente...situated between the Mission and Las Peñasquitos; it was used as a vineyard, orchard, garden, etc.;

it was so called after an Indian named Clemente who had charge of it. *(The San Diego Union,* July 23, 1875.)

There is no record of neophyte Clemente having been "sainted." It is possible this canyon eventually became "San Clemente" from persons in the district who assumed it had been named after Orange County's San Clemente or San Clemente Island.

Saint Clemente was the third Pope of Rome, famous for discovering, through a miracle, a clear spring of water on a barren island.

SAND CREEK. A descriptive geographical feature in El Capitan district. This is a common place-name throughout the U.S.

SANDIA CANYON. (Spanish for "watermelon.") Probably a description for a place where a wild species of melon was abundant. (Located northeast from De Luz.)

SAN DIEGO: City, Bay, River. (Spanish for "Saint Didacus.") "First you must name all the towns and places which you find there," were the instructions from the king of Spain to his exploring new captains. This royal command was the king's procedural demand for claiming possession of a territory. Capt. Juan Rodriguez Cabrillo of Portugal was obeying these instructions when he sailed into today's San Diego Harbor on September 28, 1542, and named it "San Miguel" in honor of that saint's feast day. (See also under SAN MIGUEL MOUNTAIN.)

The Spanish military custom of flourish and ostentation soon would be manifested in a special place-naming ceremony: a large cross was to be erected, and mass conducted, terminating with the declaration of the special name selected — all in honor of king and empire. The captain would draw his sword in defiance of any future challenger to this Spanish claim of possession. Some of his followers might hack away at trees. Others sometimes built a heap of stones. All this pomp and ceremony was testimony to Heaven that Spanish royal possession was now established. (G. Stewart, pp. 12-13)

When explorer Vizcaino arrived at the above site of San Miguel on November 10, 1602, he named it "San Diego" in honor of the feast day of San Diego de Alcala de Heuares. Vizcaino's flagship also was named "San Diego." Either Vizcaino was ignorant of Cabrillo's earlier name-designation or he sought personal glory by pretending to have discovered a new harbor. Thus San Diego harbor was honored by the visits of two famous early explorers at different feast dates, and received back-to-back saint place-names.

From 1602 to 1769 the California sun rose and set, the Pacific surf roared and boomed, and the seasons changed — but in this spread of 167 years no new daring explorers from Spain were commissioned to set foot on California soil. By 1767, however, Spain realized it faced the risk of losing California to either Great Britain or Russia.

The Portola expedition of 1769 did not sail to California with the same courage of challenging the unknown as did Cabrillo and Vizcaino. Rather, theirs was an expedition whose purpose was to organize the control of lands that Spanish kings had long claimed as part of their empire. On June 29, 1769, Portola and his party arrived in San Diego. The establishment of a *presidio* (garrison) in San Diego was the beginning of Spanish colonization in California.

Fifty years after the arrival of Portola's expedition in 1769 the colony of San Diego had made very little progress, according to historian William Smythe in *History of San Diego:*

Up to 1819, the military force at the Presidio was about fifty-five men, besides a detail of twenty-five soldiers at the Mission, and twenty invalids living at Los Angeles or on ranches. In that year the number was increased to one hundred and ten men, and in 1820 the total population of the district was about four hundred and fifty. In August of that year the British whaler Discovery put in for provisions – the only foreign ship for several years. . . .

At the close of the Spanish rule, San Diego was still a sleepy little military post on a far frontier. The fortifications were dilapidated, the soldiers in rags and destined to lose their arrears of pay, and the invalids their pensions. The missions had large possessions, but were impoverished by the enforced support of the military for many years. Commerce was dead and agriculture had scarcely begun. (p. 96)

San Diego (Saint Didacus) was a fifteenth-century Franciscan who performed missionary work in the Canary Islands for his religious order. San Diego died in the convent of Alcala in Castile, Spain.

The Indian name for San Diego harborside and district was "Wee-ilsh-nee-wah," meaning "place of many fleas."

SAN DIEGO COUNTY. In January 1850, the first legislature of California appointed a committee to determine the definition and derivation of the names of the original 27 counties (including San Diego). The committee's report was printed in English and Spanish.

A California historian delineated the historical status of San Diego County soon after American occupation:

In 1850 and for a number of years after, there was no settlement in San Diego County outside of the city that could be called a town. At each of the large ranchos there was a small settlement made up of servants and vaqueros and their families Some of these were designated as precincts when a general election was called, and at a few some one acted as a justice of the peace. . . .The history of the county and the city are identical for nearly two decades. The back country so often spoken of was undeveloped and the very few events that happened at points back from the bay are unimportant. . .(J.M. Guinn, *A History of California And An Extended History of Its Southern Coast Counties,* Vol. I, p. 262)

The first U.S. census in 1850 documented Guinn's interpretation: it reported 798 county residents (excluding Indians) with 650 residents in San Diego City and 148 in the county. Therefore it would be plausible to conclude that until 1870 the history of San Diego County largely was a history of the city.

Historic political note: The day and way of a political convention in San Diego County possibly afforded an opportunity for frontier Californians to express their individualism. *The San Diego Union,* January 23, 1869, reported the following San Luis Rey district political convention:

Conn was unanimously endorsed by the party for Senator. Blunt Couts nominated for Assemblyman by acclamation; during the excitement four men dragged out and laid on Dr. Thompson's dissecting table; James McCoy tossed in a blanket; John McIntire thrown overboard; G. Estudillo hit on the head with a bundle of scrip; M. Mannasse had to leave on his fast horse; G. Pendleton carried off by the San Luis Rey villains when Bush's name from San Diego was mentioned, the scene that followed beggars all description: curry-combs, jack knives, pistols, barley sacks, boats, Gorham speeches, bridle-bitts (sic), in fact everything that the unterrified had about them was thrown at the speaker. Through some friends at Ballena, he was gently laid out under the Rostrum. Aguadiente was used as a restorative. Meeting adjourned amid terrible carnage.

Historical cost-of-living note:

The cost of living in San Diego County (1887) differs but little from prices ruling in the older States. Hardware, groceries, dry goods, and farming implements can be bought here at a very slight advance on Eastern rates, the only difference being the freight charges. Meats, fruits, vegetables are rather cheaper than in Eastern markets. The cost of building substantial, comfortable houses is about as reasonable here as in the East. A nice, five-room cottage can be built for $800, and larger houses at from $175 to $250 per room. From $2000 - $3000 will build a handsome 10-room or 12-room residence. . . .Wages for ordinary day laborers range from $1.50 to $2.50 per day; harvest hands (with board) $25 to $30 per month; skilled workmen from $3 to $5 per day; clerks, accountants, and salesmen from

$50 to $150 per month, according to ability and experience. (Douglas Gunn, *Picturesque San Diego,* p. 95)

SAN DIEGUITO RIVER. (Spanish for "little San Diego" River.) There is no certainty about the meaning of this place-name. Some believe it was derived from St. Didacus de Alcala (or after San Diego). Others declared it was derived from St. James the Lesser (St. James of La Marca, Ancona, Italy), a Franciscan priest who died before Columbus discovered America.

The pueblo of San Dieguito long existed as an Indian *rancheria* (village). In 1845 Juan Maria Osuna, the first *alcalde* (mayor) of San Diego, received this rancho as a land grant, and he retained its original name. The river flowed along the southern part of the grant. Rancho Santa Fe is the present name for San Dieguito Rancho. (J.D.) (See also under RANCHO SANTA FE.)

SANDSTONE CANYON. A descriptive place-name for this geographical site in Anza-Borrego Desert.

SAN ELIJO LAGOON. (Spanish for "Saint Alexius.") The Portola expedition camped here on July 16, 1769. Padre Crespi named it for this saint whose feast day was July 17, a fifth-century holy Christian reported to have been proclaimed "the man of God" soon after his death.

San Elijo is one of the few place-names of the Portola march of 1769 still in existence. (G.) (See also under CHRISTIANITOS CANYON.)

SAN FELIPE: Settlement, Creek, Hills, Valley. (Spanish for "Saint Philip.") Possibly named for Holy Philip, a first-century saint who was martyred in Asia Minor. (G.)

Explorer Fages named this site when he camped in Ranchita district with his party in 1782. The name soon was applied to a creek, valley, and Indian *rancheria.* In 1846 Pio Pico issued the Rancho San Felipe land grant. Other explorers, missionaries, adventurers, gold-seekers, and emigrant wagons traveled through San Felipe district, on a route from Yuma to San Diego. (D.)

Today's Scissors Crossing is a part of the former San Felipe Rancho. (See also under SENTENAC CANYON.)

SAN FRANCISCO PEAK. (See under AGUA HEDIONDA.)

SAN LUIS REY: Settlement, River. (Spanish for "St. Louis, King.") In 1769 the Portola expedition rested at this site on their northward march to Monterey. Padre Crespi named it "San Juan Capistrano." He noted that the location was an excellent place for a mission. However, San Juan Capistrano Mission eventually became located some distance farther north.

In 1798 Padre Lasuer founded San Luis Rey Mission and name-designated it in honor of Louis IX, King of France. The mission was the eighteenth of the California chain of missions. Because of its large and magnificent church, it was known as "the king of the missions." Its lands and livestock were among the most extensive in California, with almost 60,000 head of cattle, and an annual grain yield of about 13,000 bushels. It was believed that this mission converted at least 7000 Indians (who were known as "Luiseños.") (J.D., W.D.)

The Indian name for this area was "Jacayme," which translates as "pleasant view." *(The San Diego Union,* March 7, 1882.)

SAN MARCOS: Town, Creek, Mountains. (Spanish for "St. Mark.") Before 1800 El Valle San Marcos was the general name for Vista and Escondido. These valleys were claimed and used for cattle grazing by San Luis Rey Mission. In 1840 the land grant Los Vallecitos de San Marcos Rancho was awarded to Jose Maria Alvarado. (P. Rush, p. 21)

In the 1880s the San Marcos Land Company bought Rancho San Marcos for $223,000 and prepared a townsite about two and one-half miles west of the present town. Houses, stores, and a post office were built. By 1892 there were 87 registered voters in the settlement. In 1901 the little new town was abandoned. It moved to its present site, for that was where the Santa Fe Railroad had constructed its depot. *(The San Diego Union,* June 2, 1968.)

Before the end of the nineteenth century the valley here was composed of three separate communities: San Marcos, Barham to the west, and Richland to the east. By 1900 the place-name of Barham had vanished, and the post offices of Richland and San Marcos had combined to become its present name-designation. The creek and mountains apparently were named after the land grant. (There were several saints named Mark. It is not clear which saint's name was applied here. However, a ninth-century St. Mark, the evangelist, apostle, and martyr, was popular with Jesuit fathers.)

The modern town of San Marcos now occupies about 80 percent of the original land grant.

SAN MATEO: Creek, Canyon, Point. (Spanish for "St. Matthew.") Mission Juan Capistrano quite early serviced San Mateo *rancheria* (village) at the "Point" (adjacent to present San Onofre). The creek and canyon were probably named after the *rancheria.*

San Mateo, holy evangelist and apostle, apparently was among the favorite saints of Jesuit padres.

SAN ONOFRE: Canyon, Creek, Mountain. (Spanish for "St. Onuphrius.") This saint of Egyptian origin was a fourth-century hermit who lived in the desert for 60 years, never uttering a word except in prayer.

A land grant of 1836 was titled "Santa Margarita y San Onofro." San Onofro Rancho was considered to have been administered by San Juan Capistrano Mission as early as 1828. The canyon and mountain are in the San Onofre region.

The Sante Fe Railroad named its depot here "San Onofre." (G.)

SAN PASQUAL: Valley, Indian Reservation. (Spanish for "St. Paschal.") The valley apparently takes its name from an early Indian pueblo under the administration of San Diego Mission. The name of "San Pascual" was bestowed by the early Franciscan padres.

St. Paschal was a Spanish peasant, born in 1540. He became a Franciscan padre famous for his devoted courtesy and charity to the poor. (G., Ha.)

San Pasqual Indian Reservation comprises almost 1400 acres. The preserve was established in 1910 for the Pasqual natives who were dispossessed in 1875 from their original village. An article in *The San Diego Union,* January 23, 1972, reported 19 residents on the reservation.

The Diegueño Indian place-name for this district was "Aurl-mo-culsch-culsch" (place of a big rock on a smaller rock). (Ha.)

Historical memo: San Pasqual Valley is a memorable name in California history because of the short battle here in 1846 between General Kearny's forces and General Pico's band of California Rangers. (See also under MULE HILL.)

SANTA CATARINA SPRINGS. (Spanish for "St. Catherine.") The Anza expedition arrived at Collins Valley on the feast day of this saint. It was here that Father Garces carved a message on the willow tree reporting difficulty with the Indians. (H. Parker, p. 26)

SANTA MARGARITA: Creek, River, Mountains, Rancho. (Spanish for "St. Margaret.") The history of this place-name began with Father Crespi of the Portola expedition in 1769. The party arrived at this river site on the feast day of St. Margaret, and Crespi designated its name. (St. Margaret was a third-century Antioch maiden who was martyred during the reign of Caius Diocletian.)

119

The San Luis Rey Mission (near Oceanside) was founded in 1798, and its Franciscan padres controlled grazing lands in what are now San Diego, Riverside, and Orange Counties. San Onofre y Santa Margarita Rancho was a part of these mission holdings. Secularization made it possible for Pio and Andres Pico to receive a land grant of over 133,000 acres (now titled "Santa Margarita y Las Flores Rancho"), the largest grant in the county. The Picos were a prominent California family; Pio Pico was the last governor before American conquest. (J.D., Ha.)

Today the greater part of this huge grant is owned by the federal government. At a cost of $4,000,000 the U.S. government in 1942 purchased 132,000 acres and created the largest Marine training base in the world. Its original ranch house of 1828 is a relic of the earlier Spanish period, and it has been the traditional residence of Marine commanders. Camp Pendleton comprises 195 square miles and includes a beach front of 17 miles. (P.W. Brackett, p. 37)

Historical military memo: The ranch for a short period was General Pico's headquarters for his regiment of Californios. It's a fair conjecture that General Pico could have held a council of war here under a large oak tree in preparation for his eventual encounter with General Kearny in San Pasqual Valley. Almost 100 years later the U.S. Marines of Camp Pendleton were to receive training on this same ranch, and Marines were to be trained here through three wars.

The creek and mountains were named after the river. (See also under CAMP PENDLETON, LAS FLORES, and JOFEGAN.)

SANTA MARIA CREEK. Located on and named for Santa Maria Rancho. This ranch was a land grant in 1833 of over 17,000 acres in a valley that before secularization was the property of San Diego Mission. The present town of Ramona is situated in the eastern part of this earlier rancho, and it is the commercial center for this district. (P. Rush, pp. 75-77) (See also under RAMONA and PAUMA.)

SANTA ROSA MOUNTAINS. This geographical feature lies in Riverside and San Diego counties. It is probably named for the Rancho Santa Rosa land grant of 1846.

According to Nellie Van De Grift Sanchez, Santa Rosa had an unusual history:

> An interesting story is told of Santa Rosa de Lima, said to be the only canonized female saint of the new world. She was born at Lima, in Peru, and was distinguished for her hatred of vanity, and her great austerity, carrying these characteristics to such an extreme that she destroyed her beautiful complexion with a compound of pepper and quicklime. When her mother commanded her to wear a wreath of roses, she so arranged it that it was in truth a crown of thorns. Her food consisted principally of bitter herbs, and she maintained her parents by her labor, working all day in her garden and all night with her needle. The legend relates that when Pope Clement X was asked to canonize her he refused, exclaiming, 'An Indian woman a saint? That may happen when it rains roses!' Instantly a shower of roses began to fall in the Vatican, and did not cease until the Pope was convinced of his error. (N. Sanchez, *Spanish and Indian Place Names of California,* p. 178)

SANTA TERESA VALLEY. (Spanish for "St. Theresa.") Pioneer William Cole homesteaded in Mesa Grande area in 1850, naming his ranch after the Santa Teresa Spring. No information is available for the saint-naming of this spring. It is possible that an Indian *rancheria* here had been named "Santa Teresa" by San Diego Mission. (J.D.)

Santa Teresa, born in Spain in 1515, devoted herself to reforming the order of Mount Carmel. She revived the earlier order's requirement of barefootedness, and was honored for her literary talent.

SANTA YSABEL: Settlement, Creek, Peak, Valley, Indian Reservation. (Spanish for "St. Isabella.") Originally an Indian village named "El-cua-nan" (place of twisted earth pushed up by growing vegetation). In 1795 Padre Mariner and Sgt. Grijalva led an exploring party into the mountains of this district. They found this region fertile, scenic, and well-populated with friendly and peaceful Indians. Father Mariner named the place for Santa Ysabel. The report of the padre and the sergeant to San Diego Mission included the recommendation that a chapel *(asistencia)* be established here. Thereupon a chapel was begun in 1818.

The Acts of Secularization dispossessed San Diego Mission of this land, and in 1844 Rancho Santa Ysabel became a land grant to Jose Ortega and his son-in-law, Edward Stokes, an award of over 17,000 acres. (P. Rush, pp. 50-58)

By 1889 the settlement of Santa Ysabel was only a small townsite. It never enjoyed the boom growth of neighboring settlements.

The creek, peak, valley, and Indian Reservation are named after the Santa Ysabel *asistencia* of 1818. The reservation now comprises about 2000 acres and it had 127 Indian residents in 1972.

Historical note: In 1887 writer Theodore Van Dyke described the Santa Ysabel district as follows:

> . . .at an elevation of 3,000 feet we come into the valley of the Rancho Santa Ysabel. This is the central valley of the rancho, containing, with its branches and slopes, some 4000 acres of fine land, but used with the adjoining hills only for stock range, dairying, and cheese-making. Here are still more evidences of a heavy rainfall. Springs are almost on every hill-side, little streams in every ravine, while nearby across the center runs a creek that in the driest time of the year has a large stream of the purest water. All these surrounding hills, like the main valley, are splendid stock range, affording abundance of feed. (T. Van Dyke, p. 36)

Van Dyke's description of almost 100 years ago is accurate today, for there has been little transformation in this region. Climate and geography are unchanged, and the land is still devoted chiefly to cattle-raising and dairying. (See also under PAUMA.)

SANTEE: Town, Lakes. The district originally was referred to as "Cowles Ranch," after George Cowles, a prominent early rancher. Sometime after his death his widow married Milton Santee, a real estate developer. When the townsite here was ready to receive a post office, many persons preferred to designate the name of "Cowles." Mrs. Santee, however, urged that the name of her second husband was more desirable. The Postal Department in Washington thereupon helped honor her second husband. He became its postmaster. (Ha.)

The community years earlier had been named "Fanita," after its first postmistress, Mrs. Fanita McCoon. (G.)

SAN VICENTE: Creek, Mountain, Reservoir, Valley. (Spanish for "St. Vincent.") The name-designation of a Mexican land grant in 1845 was "Cañada de San Vicente y Mesa del Barona." Don Juan Bautista Lopez was the first grantee. (Ha.) Part of the ranch's title honored Padre Barone who served at San Diego Mission 1798-1810.

For over 100 years the district has had a history of cattle-raising, dairying, mining, and goat-raising.

In 1932 the Barona Valley was purchased by the federal government to provide a new homesite for the El Capitan Indians who had to abandon their ancestral homesite in El Capitan Reservoir district. (P. Rush, pp. 99-100) (See also under BARONA.)

SAN YSIDRO. Town, Creek, Mountains. (Spanish for "St. Isadore.") San Ysidro was the Spanish patron saint of farming, and this name was designated several times in

San Diego county: for a creek, Indian *rancheria* (village), two mountain ranges, and a town.

The San Ysidro *asistencia* near Warner Springs was a branch of San Diego Mission, and it dates back to 1836. The creek and mountains were designated after the nearby San Ysidro Indian village and rancho. (G.)

The San Ysidro community at the Mexican border south from San Diego, and just opposite Tijuana, probably was named after a ranch of the same name across the border in Mexico. The San Diego Mission established a chapel here about 1818.

In 1909, William E. Smythe organized and promoted his "Little Landers" colony at San Ysidro district, an experiment in back-to-the-soil livelihood for families of limited means — even for families with no farming experience — who sought to abandon the pressures of urbanized living. Smythe's small prospectus booklet stated:

> The colony was born of the needs of these strenuous times. Thousands of people are weary of the rush, turmoil, and uncertainty of the city. . . .

Smythe published a small magazine which he declared to be devoted to "the art of deriving a comfortable subsistance from the smallest area of soil" (a quotation from Abraham Lincoln). Smythe earnestly believed that "a man can make a living from a little land — from so little land as he can use to best advantage without hiring help." (Herbert Hensley, *Memoirs,* Supplement.) The colony was successful until a catastrophic flood in 1916 destroyed its farms. Its lands remained waterlogged for a long time, discouraging the colonists from any further agricultural efforts. *(The San Diego Union,* Aug. 30, 1958.)

The small remaining business settlement of San Ysidro gradually prospered as a commercial and tourist way station between the U.S. and Baja California, Mexico.

SECRET CANYON. This folk-type name designation in Descanso district implies a site that is not readily accessible.

SENTENAC: Canyon, Creek. Place-named for brothers Pete and Paul Sentenac who homesteaded here in the 1880s as desert stockmen in the Anza-Borrego region. Paul Sentenac also raised sheep and goats here for several years. The canyon had been referred to as "San Felipe" before the Frenchmen took possession. (J.D.) (See also under SAN FELIPE.)

SEQUAN: Indian Reservation, Peak. (Indian for "yellow primrose.") An application for the land grant "Secuan" was recorded in 1835, and an Indian *rancheria* "Socouan" is mentioned in 1836 as an appendage of San Diego Mission. (G.) The Bureau of Indian Affairs, however, has recorded this site as "Sycuan."

The reservation is very small, consisting of only 641 acres, less than 10 miles east from El Cajon, with 31 residents. Because of its limited size, most of these residents prefer to earn their living in the district, and use the reservation chiefly for homesites. (L. Swain, *Story of the Indians of San Diego County*, pp. 131-132)

In 1880 Helen Hunt Jackson made an inspection visit here which she reported in *Century of Dishonor:*

The Sequan Indians are a small band of Diegueño Indians living in a rift of the hills on one side of the Sweetwater Cañon, about 20 miles from San Diego. There are less than 50 of them. They are badly off, having for the last 10 years been more and more encroached on by white settlers, until now they can keep no cattle, and have little cultivable land left.

There is a small reservation of one section set off for them, but the lines were never pointed out to them, and they said they did not know whether it were true that they had a reservation or not. As nearly as we could determine, this village is within the reservation lines; and if it is, some of the fields which have been recently taken away from the Indians by the whites must be also. . . .These Indians are much dispirited and demoralized, and wretchedly poor. (p. 500)

SEVENTEEN PALMS SPRING. A descriptive designation in northeast San Diego County just west of the Imperial County line. This oasis was a well-known watering place in Borrego Badlands in desert history.

Earlier desert dwellers readily augmented folk tales of fabulous mines and "thirst-crazed men and animals" that became legendary features of this oasis.

According to desert authority Horace Parker, the magnesium sulfate in this salty spring is of an extremely laxative nature.

In 1899 an ethnobotanist wrote:

> But the most striking botanical feature of the desert is its cañons of palms. . .many of them rise forty feet high, covered with the persistent bases and sheaths of dead leaves while at the top they are crowned with long, graceful fronds. . . .the approach to these spots [palm] is sudden and the sight most unexpected and amazing. Such luxuriant, tropical vegetation would never be looked for in the midst of such sterile surroundings. The pools of water impounded in the bottoms of the cañons explain their presence. Many strange theories have been evoked to account for the existence here of these stately trees. . . .the same species are to be found in the Cocopah and Sierra Madre mountains of Lower California, Guadaloupe Island, and the Mexican mainland. (David P. Barrows, *The Ethno-Botany of the Coahuilla Indians of Southern California,* p. 32)

SHEEP CANYON. Was this a place where wild sheep ranged? Or was it a site of a sheep ranch? This locale is a side canyon off Coyote Canyon in Borrego Desert.

SHEPHERD CANYON. Was this a folk place-name? Or was this canyon in Miramar area used for sheep grazing at one time by San Diego Mission?

126

SHINGLE SPRING. Long-time resident Mrs. A. Bergman recalled that the abundant cedars here furnished homesteaders with shingle material for their roofs. (Located in Los Coyotes region.)

SHORT WASH. Park Ranger Jack Welch named this site in Borrego Badlands for Orville G. Short, one of the first fulltime park patrol rangers.

SIMMONS CANYON. A personal place-name whose identity remains unknown. (Located in Laguna Mountains area.)

SKUNK SPRING. Such a name-designation could be merely descriptive of the water's peculiar quality, or a folk-type appellation for an event that occurred here involving one or more skunks. (Located in Barona district.)

SKYE VALLEY. The McLean brothers migrated from Scotland and homesteaded in this valley. They transferred the name of Skye from their land of birth and designated it for this valley north of Barrett Lake. (B.)

SLAUGHTERHOUSE CANYON. Located northwest from Lakeside, this place-name probably was designated for a meat-processing establishment at this site.

SLEEPY HOLLOW. An apparent borrowed or transferred place-name that perhaps intended to describe a feeling of ease and contentment. Ranger Jack Welch reported this Borrego name-designation may have been the idea of Harry Woods, an early Borrego resident.

SMOKE TREE WASH. This descriptive place-name designates a desert wash near Font's Point in Anza-Borrego district.

SMUGGLERS CANYON. A descriptive place-name for a locale near Agua Caliente Springs. Smuggling was considered an honorable enough enterprise in earlier days on both sides of the U.S. border — if you didn't get caught. Profitable contraband for Mexican smugglers at one time were Chinese laborers, who hoped to work in desert mines in the Colorado River development, as fishermen out of San Diego harbor, or on the railroad.

SOLANA BEACH. (Spanish for "sunshine.") Place-named by Col. Ed Fletcher in 1923 when he laid out its townsite. "Lockwood Mesa" was its earlier name.

Mr. and Mrs. Herbert Estes were its first settlers in 1912, and Mr. Estes is credited with having been the first farmer to raise potatoes in the district. He also was able "to regularly shoot rabbits, coyotes, and rattlesnakes" from his front porch. (J.D.)

The development of water projects on the San Luis Rey and San Dieguito Rivers stimulated settlement on the coast from Del Mar to Oceanside in the 1920s. The construction of Lake Hodges encouraged Fletcher to develop this townsite.

Mr. Fletcher also applied Spanish names to the streets of Solana Beach. (J.D.)

SOLEDAD MOUNTAIN. (Spanish for "solitude.") The first mention of this La Jolla site was by Anza, whose expedition rested here on January 10, 1776. Anza's diary states that the Indians encountered in this area had been Christianized by San Diego Mission, and it was place-named "Rancheria de Nuestra Señora de la Soledad" (Village of Our Lady of Solitude). In 1838 a Mexican land grant in this area, referred to as "Rancho Soledad," was granted to Francisco Maria Alvarado. Apparently the mountain was named after the Indian *rancheria.* (G., J.D.) (See also under SORRENTO.)

According to researcher Gudde, this Spanish word for "solitude" was frequently designated in Spanish colonial times. (G.)

SOMBRERO PEAK. The upper part of this elevation in Anza-Borrego Desert suggests a sombrero shape.

SORRENTO SETTLEMENT. Place-named after the well-known Italian city by the San Diego Town and Land Company in 1887. The site was on part of the earlier Rancho Soledad. (J.D.)

Situated on a plateau below and south from Torrey Pines Grade, lots were advertised at $100 each, and the land was described as so unusual that one could "grow anything in the world with or without irrigation." *(The San Diego Union,* Oct. 1, 1887.) See also under SOLEDAD MOUNTAIN.)

SOURDOUGH SPRING. The origin of this apparent folk-name remains unexplained. It implies the idea of prospecting or mining. (Located in Palomar district.)

SOUTH FORK ALDER CANYON. A descriptive place-name in the northwest corner of Anza-Borrego Desert.

It is a plausible conjecture that the use of "fork" (branch) for a canyon may have been the idea of a former gold-rush miner. According to George Stewart, California's eminent place-name scholar, "fork" as a descriptive term was often applied to California rivers, and this designation was common during the gold rush of 1849:

> The whole life of the Forty-Niners was involved with rivers. They found rich digging on the gravel-bars, and must have running water to work their cradles and rockers. In exploring the country, they kept close to the rivers, and since most of them landed at San Francisco and the gold-country was on the westward slope, they advanced into that country upstream, just as their ancestors had advanced into the Alleghenies. So they frequently came to a place where the river, to a man looking upstream, seemed to divide into two forks, almost equal. This was the more likely because everybody was in a great hurry, and they were all passing on to another place, never settling down. So even if some man named a stream, he might not stay there long enough to tell the next man what it was.
>
> Most of the rivers had a North, South, and Middle Fork. Beyond that was a second degree in such names as The

129

North Fork of the Middle Fork of the American River, which might be clipped to North-Middle American. Some streams went into the third degree as in The East Fork of the North Fork of the North Fork of the American, and the delightfully explicit West Fork of the South Fork of the North Fork of the San Joaquin. (G. Stewart, p. 267)

Hence the language transmission of "fork" from river to canyon. In the eastern part of the U.S, "fork" had been applied largely to the branching of a road.

SOUTH FORK BORREGO PALM CANYON. (See under PALM CANYON and SOUTH FORK ALDER CANYON.)

SOUTH FORK SHEEP CANYON. (See under SHEEP CANYON and SOUTH FORK ALDER CANYON.)

SOUTH MESA. A descriptive place-name for a flat elevation in Anza-Borrego Desert, southeast from Agua Caliente Springs.

SPANGLER PEAK. This elevation's name-designation (south from Ramona) remains unexplained.

SPLIT MOUNTAIN. An apt descriptive place-name for a mountain with a cleft and gateway at desert level, located east from Agua Caliente Springs. Indians long ago lived nearby until an earthquake destroyed their water supply. Desert lore included tales of prospectors lost in the maze of side canyons in this mountainous badland. (J.D., B.)

In *California Desert Trails,* writer J.S. Chase described his route through Split Mountain with a companion in 1918:

In we dived; and, indeed, to plunge into one of these mazes is much like diving into unknown water. . . .In and out, up and down, we went for hours, scrambling up and sliddering down. Now and then we left the horses and climbed out to get our bearings afresh. . .We reached at length a rim from which we looked out over a still more intricate piece of country. With a sweep of the hand my companion remarked, "There's the worst stretch of country I know, and I know most all the bad layouts from Idaho down.

More men have got lost in that mass of stuff than any other place I ever saw, and most of them are there yet. Miner's Hell I call it, easy to get in and the devil to get out. Well, I know where we are anyhow. I wasn't sure before, but now there'll be some monuments if we can find 'em, so I reckon we'll get through."

It was a remarkable sight. Imagine a cauldron of molten rock, miles wide, thrown by earthquake shock into the complexity of a choppy sea and then struck immovable. (p. 256)

SPLIT ROCK. A descriptive place-name for a geographical formation east of Earthquake Valley in Anza-Borrego Desert.

SPOOK CANYON. (See under HARMONY GROVE.)

SPRING CANYON. A descriptive place-name for a canyon with a stream, located in El Cajon Valley and east from Santee.

SPRING VALLEY. This descriptive name-designation originally was a watering place which the Indians referred to as "Meti" or "Neti" (meaning unknown). In 1775 the San Diego Mission recorded the Indian *rancheria* here as "Los Fuentes de San Jorge" (Springs of St. George). After secularization, this valley became in 1846 a parcel of the vast land grant to the Arguello family. Under American occupation a ranch was established here by Augustus Ensworth (1850), sold to Capt. Rufus K. Porter (1865), and later sold to Hubert H. Bancroft, the famous California historian (1885). The place was now designated as "Bancroft Ranch," and it was here that the historian did some of his writing. (J.D.)

The Golden Era of July 1887 described Bancroft in the following manner:

Mr. Bancroft is 55 years of age, in vigorous health, and possesses a more than common endurance. He usually writes standing. . . .His desk is accordingly made about breast high, and close beside it is a circular table, about

131

eight feet in diameter, fitted with a revolving top, on which he arranges his authorities, turning the table top round as he requires them. He frequently stands at his desk for 11 or 12 hours.

In a letter to *The San Diego Union* in 1878, Capt. Porter explained the name-designation for this valley:

I like Spanish, Mexican, or Indian names, and would not have changed the name to 'Spring Valley' as far as I was concerned, but my folks wanted some other; hence the name.

A "What's Happening in Spring Valley" news column in *The San Diego Union,* June 24, 1885, reported some daily conditions and routines of life in the Valley:

The South Chollas road is now mostly used instead of the Cajon road, the latter being so terribly worn and cut up by incessant travel. . . .The road up and down this valley which was looked at a long time ago by road viewers, has had nothing done to it, and will probably not be touched till the Mission lands are divided. . . .

Wild cats and coyotes are again heard from after a long rest. They have latterly been giving attention to the poultry of David Little on the river near the foot of San Miguel Mountain. . . .

The great abundance of cottontail rabbits (in this valley) has saved the poultry from being raided. Our neighbor, George Powell the elder, can take the cake on rabbit shooting. He makes weekly trips to San Diego in his light wagon, takes his breech loading gun along, and kills going and returning from 20 to 40 of the little chaps every trip. His young son Burt accompanies him, picks up the animals going in, and peddles them around town. He killed 38 last Saturday. Early in the morning and late in the afternoon is the time to see and shoot the most.

T. M. Turner was taking a look at the valley several days ago, and a gentleman whom I do not know was with him. Real estate men don't come out this way often nowadays; too much to do in the city.

In 1974 Spring Valley ranked eighth in population in the county.

SQUAW PEAK. Ralph L. Caine in *Lost Desert Gold* reported a long-time prospector's legend about an Indian squaw who claimed she found gold nuggets at the toes of this butte. Manifestly the persistence of this legend caused much prospecting of every inch of this low elevation. Although no gold was ever unearthed, the legend continued to lure gold-seekers to try their luck at this site north from Ocotillo Wells.

STARVATION MOUNTAIN. (See under MULE HILL.)

STOKES VALLEY. An apparent personal name (in Barrett Lake area) whose identity remains unknown.

STONEWALL: Peak, Mine. An apt descriptive name-designation for a huge wall of granite in Cuyamaca Valley, topping a rugged single mountain and suggesting a crown of stone.

Historical note: The famous Stonewall Jackson gold mine was discovered in 1870 and named for the Civil War rebel general. Although the Civil War had ended, apparently the Southern and Northern miners bristled or fought at the mention of the General's name. In the interest of peace — and industrial efficiency — the mine's name was shortened to "Stonewall," thereby making the peak a geographical partner of the mine. (J.D.)

STORM CANYON. According to Borrego State Park Ranger Alfred Welcome, this narrow canyon is a "draw" for winds that often blow through canyon washes in mild sandstorm form.

STUART: Settlement, Spring. Stuart Settlement (Oceanside area) was named in 1908 for E.B. Stuart, Santa Fe Railroad agent. (J.D.)

Stuart Spring (Ranchita district) was named for a desert prospector who lost his way years ago in Grapevine Canyon. His aimless wandering led him to a spring, where he was rescued two days later by Alfred

133

Wilson, desert rancher and prospector. "I named the spring for him," Wilson recalled with a chuckle, "but I can't remember whether Stuart was his first or last name!" (Borrego resident Alfred Wilson.)

SUNCREST. A descriptive site northeast from El Cajon. John McCutcheon owned this settlement of 360 acres under the name of Juanita Ranch. He sold the land in 1924 to Allen Houser and Ray Coast, who planned to develop a recreational and cabin resort community, offering 25 by 100-foot lots for $40. By 1933 over 300 cabins had been constructed on these lots.

The remains of Indian artifacts in the area indicated the existence of an earlier native campsite. (J.D.)

SUNDAY SCHOOL FLATS. Pioneer Theodore O. Bailey arrived in Palomar district with his family in 1887. He was responsible for establishing the first public school and also the first Sunday school at this site. Open-air worship meetings in conjunction with the religious school suggested the apt folk-name of "Sunday School Flats."

Bailey's "first" as an established settler was the piano he hauled up Palomar grade. (W.D.)

SUNNYSIDE. This descriptive site near Chula Vista was named by J.C. Frisbie, who enjoyed its location and exposure. Frisbie came to San Diego in 1876 in search of a desirable place to improve his health, and homesteaded in this region. He subdivided his land, maintained a 246-acre ranch, and restored his health. Frisbie was considered an expert farmer, extremely successful in cultivating grapes and citrus fruits. (J.D.)

SUNSET: Mountain, Wash. A descriptive name-designation located southwest from Ocotillo Wells.

SUNSHINE: Mountain, Summit. Obviously place-named for its location and climate. The mountain is southwest from Julian, and the summit is east from Palomar Mountain.

SUPERSTITION MOUNTAIN. According to State Park Ranger Alfred Welcome (Anza-Borrego Desert), local Indians once believed that spirits of ancient Indians came to life here after sunset, causing rumbling noises as they emerged from the mountain's many caves. The natives regarded this site with great fear and avoided its environs.

SURPRISE: Canyon, Grove. Located in Sweeney Pass, this folk-name speaks for itself.

SUTHERLAND RESERVOIR. Ed Fletcher place-named the dam for pioneer John P. Sutherland who came to Ramona as a pioneer and eventually became a real estate developer in that district. The dam's construction spread out over 25 years, due to political futility and public indifference. (Vertical File: Dams — "Sutherland," San Diego Historical Society, Serra Museum Library.)

SWARTZ CANYON. A geographic site of a homesteader whose identity remains unexplained. (Located in Ramona district.)

SWEENEY: Canyon, Pass. Lieutenant Thomas William Sweeny (sic) was regarded as an unusually brave soldier and officer. He was stationed at Fort Yuma in the 1850s, and his name and military reputation soon became known in the Carrizo district. Part of his authority was to protect emigrant wagons on their way to — or through — southern California.

Sweeney Canyon and Pass thus honor this officer.

SWEETWATER: River, Reservoir, Spring. The earlier Spanish name for the stream was "Agua Dulce," a name-designation shown as early as 1800 on an old map of San Diego district. An article in *The San Diego Union*, January 23, 1875, delineates the river with its Indian legendary background:

This river is nine miles west of the Tia Juana [river]. Its source is in the highest eastern spur of the Southern

Cuyamaca peak in some cold springs near an old Indian village called Japatia. . . .The little creek winds three miles through Green Valley. . .to make its appearance again, a clear, full stream, in July, in the little Guataj valley.

Somewhere in the dark forests of pine and oak that shade it, is the scene of a legend derived from an old Indian named Chono: Mito-pitl-pit (tall, strong man) was strong enough with one arm to pull down any one of the largest trees. He had numerous wives, always selecting them from among the youngest and best looking daughters of every family. He treated them too severely. It is told he took a distaste for the good water so easy to get in the lower valley, and forced the women continually to bring him water from the cold spring high up in the mountain of the southern peak.

This tyranny became unsupportable. His own family conspired against him. One day finding him asleep where he lived — down in the deep gorge beginning a mile below Green Valley — they bound him fast and set fire to the house. In his struggles the hills resounded with his throes. In vain! Their arrangements were well made. He perished.

Sweetwater Reservoir was completed in 1886 and takes its name from the river it impounds.

Sweetwater Spring was once advertised throughout the U.S. In addition to other curative powers, it was guaranteed to grow hair on the baldest of bald heads. Its exploitation began in 1889 when it was variously referred to as "Baldhead," "Isham's California Waters of Life," "Minwell," "Original California Water," and "Foster's Spring." By 1909 the miracle spring had been exposed by *Collier's Weekly* as "The Great American Fraud." Thereby this erstwhile famous feature recorded itself in San Diego County history as an infamous watery enterprise. (J.D.)

SYCAMORE: Canyon, Flats. A descriptive place-name of a natural feature. The canyon in Miramar region earlier had been designated by the Spanish or Mexicans as "Valle de los Alisos." The flats are located in San Pasqual area. (See also under ALISO CANYON.)

TALEGA CANYON. (Spanish for "bag" or "sack.") Probably the shape of this canyon suggested its place-name. (San Clemente area.)

TAYLOR: Creek, Spring. An apparent personal name-designation whose identity is not known. Taylor Creek empties into Loveland Reservoir. Taylor Spring is located in Cuyamaca District.

TECATE: Settlement, Peak. One reference translates this Spanish or Mexican name as "water in which the baker moistens her hands for making tortillas." Another source suggests it derives from the Mexican *tecats* (a species of gourd). (G.) The valley of Tecate was an established old Indian trail across the border. In 1833 Tecate Rancho was the name of a land grant to Don Juan Bandini. In 1837, Indian lootings and assaults in Tecate valley publicized the area as one of Indian cruelty and terror. By 1867 most of the Indians had been either slain or driven out of the area, and Yankees and Mexicans were able to settle in this valley where they cultivated fruit and vegetables. Their frontier cabins and adobe houses dotted the scenic slopes that touched the Mexican border. The site soon was nicknamed "Tecatito" (little Tecate) by the Tecate Mexicans adjacently across the border.

Tecate Peak had been a sacred mountaintop for the earlier Indians. Here went the young brave, ready for initiation into manhood, to meditate solitarily for at least one night, anticipating a vision while he slept. From such a dream the young native and his elders attempted to determine his future role as a tribal member. (J.D.)

TELEGRAPH CANYON. Named for the telegraph line that passed through the canyon in Otay area. This communication service was established in San Diego County in 1870, extending eastward to Yuma. Poles were delivered by wagons and portered into this canyon. (J.D.)

San Diego's first telegraphic communication with the rest of the world occurred on August 19, 1870. The following day *The San Diego Union* headlined "Extra!" over the following terse, matter-of-fact report:

VERY IMPORTANT NEWS! The telegraph completed to San Diego! Congratulatory Dispatches.

And the rest of this "Extra" reported datelines of news around the world with not a word of comment about how important it was for San Diego to have this "modern miracle of words" flashing through Telegraph Canyon and out to the four corners of the world.

> Historical note: In earlier days signals of importance for the townspeople were transmitted by the raising of a flag on the old lighthouse on Pt. Loma (to announce the arrival of a steamer — or a large school of whales).

TEMESCAL: Creek, Valley. (Aztec for "bath house.") Erwin Gudde reports this place-name to be derived from the Mexican usage of the word:

> The word is not of California Indian origin. . . .The primitive sweathouses. . .aroused the curiosity of the Spaniards, who applied to them the Mexican word for 'bathhouse,' *temascal.* (p. 317)

Temescal Valley and Creek are located in Lake Henshaw area. Another Temescal Creek is situated in Santa Ysabel region.

THE MESA. (Spanish for "tableland.") Located north from Jamul. Geographically, this land feature is actually a peak rather than a tableland.

THE POTRERO. (Spanish for "pasture or meadow.") South from Vallecito. (See also under POTRERO.)

THE WILLOWS. A descriptive place-name for a locale once abundant with willow trees at a stream's edge. Situated two miles east from Alpine, it was a popular cabin resort for many years.

In 1887 Frederick B. Walker brought his family to San Diego where he conducted a printing business. By 1894 he had changed his occupational interest to fruit-ranching in Alpine district. By 1896 the Walker family had established a mountain resort inn which they named "The Willows." It was an extremely successful enterprise for many years.

In the stagecoach era The Willows was popular as a stopover inn, for it took more than one day to complete a trip from Julian to San Diego.

Before the settlement of the Walker family, this site had been designated as "Alpine Berry" fields after the abundant wild berries that grew here. (J.D.)

THING VALLEY. Natelia Thing Weaver (daughter of Charles Thing) reported that the family's somewhat abstract or inanimate surname had originally been "Hogg" when the earlier family resided in Wales. A member of this "Hogg" family in Wales petitioned for a change of name, explaining to the local court that the name of "Hogg" was a frequent public embarrassment. The sympathetic judge agreed to grant a change of surname — but to what new name? Mr. Hogg replied that he was ready "for anything." The judge thereupon designated "Thing" as the new family name.

Mrs. Weaver's father and his brother came to the county in 1874, settling in a valley south from Mt. Laguna. The two brothers homesteaded cattle ranches in the present Thing Valley. It formerly had been named

139

"Hollister Valley" after an earlier sheeprancher. (June N. Summers, *Buenos Dias, Tecate,* p. 15)

THIRD WASH. This "degree" type of place-name obviously was of expedient designation. (See under SOUTH FORK ALDER CANYON.)

THOUSAND PALMS (also known as "Salvador Canyon"). This grove of native palms is in a somewhat inaccessible area in Collins Valley, in Anza-Borrego Desert. It is known that the canyon slopes at one time contained an abundance of these trees. (The number of palm trees in Thousand Palms Canyon of Riverside County was even greater.) However, cloudbursts produced rushing torrents that dislodged and cascaded boulders, smashing and uprooting many of these trees through the years. The palms often reached a height of 60 feet.

Anza's expedition to Monterey passed through this canyon. (See under SALVADOR CANYON.)

TIERRA BLANCA MOUNTAIN. (Spanish for "white land.") A descriptive designation located south from Agua Caliente Springs. Gudde reports fifteen "blanca" or "blanco" orographic features in California — and more than 60 "white" orographical sites. (p. 30 and p. 344)

TIERRA DEL SOL. (Spanish for "place of the sun.") Located east from Campo and within shouting distance of the Mexican border, this place-name on August 20, 1956, replaced the former post office name, "Hipass." (G.) (See under HIPASS.)

TIMS CANYON. Santa Ysabel Postmaster Jeff Swycoffer reported that German-born Mr. Tims homesteaded in this district at the turn of the century.

TIN CAN FLAT. Such a homespun sobriquet denoted the appearance and location of a popular picnic spot on Boucher Hill. (Palomar.)

TORREY PINES PARK. Name-designated by Dr. Charles Christopher Parry, for his close friend and instructor, Dr. John Torrey.

An eminent U.S. botanist of the last century, Dr. Parry was appointed by President Polk in 1849 to serve as botanist for the U.S.-Mexican International Boundary Commission. Parry had been ordered to make a study of reported coal deposits on the ocean bluff south of Torrey Pines Park site. He discovered this unique species of pine tree during his coal investigation. In his report to his superiors, Dr. Parry wrote:

> The bulk of the tree growth here is mainly confined to a series of high broken cliffs and deeply indented ravines on the bold head-lands over-looking the sea south of Soledad Valley and within the corporate limits of the town of San Diego. Here, within a radius of not more than half a mile, this singular species may be seen to the best advantage, clinging to the face of crumbling yellowish sandstone or shooting up in more graceful form its scant foliage in the shelter of the deep ravine, bathed with frequent sea fog. One of the finest specimens seen reaches a height of nearly 50 feet and shows a trunk 18 inches in diameter at base.

Researcher John Davidson expressed the regret that the park had not been designated as "Parry Pines Park" to honor this eminent botanist. (J.D., W.D.)

TOURMALINE QUEEN MOUNTAIN. Named after a tourmaline mine in Pala district, one of the diverse gem mines of San Diego County that has a history of discovery, success, and human interest. Earlier settlers reported that Indian and white children traded for candy the pretty pink stones they found in their roamings. Emissaries of the Empress of China in the 1880s annually came to purchase for her only pink tourmaline, highly prized by the Chinese.

Tourmaline is a semi-precious mineral gemstone that is crystallized over millions of years in protected pockets of earth. The gemstone is still being mined in San Diego County; only Brazil and East Africa rank ahead of the county in tourmaline deposits. *(San Diego Union,* July 15, 1973.)

TRAGEDY SPRINGS. This folk-form of place-name in Laguna district was designated after a child was murdered at this site in the 1950s.

TRAVERTINE WASH. A descriptive place-name for the porous and honeycombed rock (tufa) present in northeast Anza-Borrego Desert. This interesting and unusual geological site was first described in 1853 by William Phipps Blake, government geologist for the Railroad Survey group of 1853. The federal administration had commissioned the group to explore for a railroad route from the Mississippi to the Pacific Ocean. Geologist Blake was dubbed "Father of the Colorado Desert" because of his important report on this desert area.

TROUTMAN MOUNTAIN. An apparent personal place-name whose identity is not known. (East of Cuyamaca Reservoir.)

TRUJILLO CREEK. Long-time resident Abe Rodriguez of Mesa Grande area stated that he was a descendant of Gregory Trujillo, who once owned a sheep ranch near this creek. Mr. Rodriguez declared that Trujillo was the grandfather of his mother, and that both were full-blooded Indians.

TUBB CANYON. Alfred Wilson has been a stockman, prospector, and cattle rancher in Borrego Desert for many years. He recalled installing a water pipe in this canyon to supply water for his cattle. The pipe produced a small flow into the sunken wooden tub, hence its name. When asked about the name's odd spelling, Wilson chuckled, "Reckon some map fellers are poor spellers."

TULE: Canyon, Dry Lake, Creek, Springs. (From the Aztec for "cattail," "bulrush," or any similar reed.) Gudde reports more than 50 such designated places in California.

TWIN: Flats, Peaks, Lakes, Oaks. It has been an American custom to designate "twin" for geographic features that are similar or unusual — in location or in appearance. For example, "Twin Oaks" is a name-designation for two giant oak trees in a settlement north from San Marcos; Twin Lakes are quite close to one another; Twin Peaks are a prominent and easily recognized landmark in Poway Valley; and Twin Flats are adjacent sites.

UN GALLO. Stephen Betland and Juan Baptiste were two French squatters in this attractive valley east and south of Pine Valley. They were credited with being the first to raise poultry in this district about 1870. Foxes and coyotes soon decimated their flock; only an aged rooster somehow survived. The two squatters protected the lone rooster in their cabin during the night.

Mexicans in the valley now quickly nicknamed the Frenchmen's homestead "El Canyon del Gallo" (Canyon of the Rooster). Like the diminished chicken flock, this sobriquet also diminished to "Un Gallo" (one rooster).

Capt. William Emery eventually bought this valley property of 160 acres which was east from a large cliff. Mrs. Emery's preferred place-name of "Glen Cliff" for a post office station was rejected, since such a name-designation already existed in California. Thereupon the family name of Emery was made the place-name for the post office station. (J.D., W.D.) (See also under PINE VALLEY.)

UNA PALMA. (Spanish for "one palm.") This place-name aptly described a solitary palm tree site near Seventeen Palms in Anza-Borrego Desert.

VALLECITO: Valley, Creek, Mountain. (Spanish for "small valley.") This small valley in southern Anza-Borrego Desert was probably named by Don Pedros Fages in 1787 when he led an expedition against Yuma Indians. The name was often misspelled (and certainly mispronounced) in newspapers and military reports as far back as 1846 as "Vallecitos," "Valle Citon," "Viollatas," "Vallecita," "Vallicitos," and "Viacielltos." Such diverse and unordinary spelling is a reminder that Vallecito Valley at one time was an important district in county history. (J.D., W.D.)

Its fame spread through the country and is recorded in American history books as: the route of the first four-wheel Yankee wagons that were used by the Mormon battalion in 1847; the Southern Emigrant Trail; the route of the "Jackass Mail" train and Butterfield stages. (J.D.) (See under BOX CANYON.)

VALLEY CENTER. Derives its name from its geographical location in the county, and this name was so designated in the 1880s when homesteaders arrived. Its earlier name had been "Bear Valley," because of the abundant presence of these animals.

The name of Philip Stedman Sparkman has a prominent place in the valley's history. Sparkman came to the area in 1884 and operated a small store. Becoming vitally interested in Luiseño culture, he mastered their language and wrote a voluminous manuscript about Luiseño grammar and vocabulary. The University of California published his books: *Culture of the Luiseño Indians, The Religion of the Luiseño Indians of Southern California,* and *The Ethnography of the Cahuilla Indians.*

In his *Culture of the Luiseño Indians* is an account of the local Indians' custom of property rights:

> The Luiseño Indians of whom we more particularly write are those living in the valley of the San Luis Rey between Pala and San Jose Valley. These formerly occupied not only the river valley but also Palomar Mountain, and there is a tradition among them that they wandered at will over this territory; on the contrary, each band had its allotted district, in which it alone had the right to gather food and hunt. Thus each band had its tract in the San Luis Rey valley, and another on Palomar, to which it moved during the acorn-gathering season. . . .

> Each band seems to have guarded its territory with the greatest of jealousy. When questioned as to when or how the land was divided, and subdivided, the Indians say they cannot tell, that their fathers told them it has always been thus. Many of the older ones remember how they were cautioned when young never to trespass on the land of others in pursuit of game or food without permission. (p. 190)

Sparkman was an Englishman who had no linguistic training, yet he mastered the Luiseño language. He became an authority on their culture, and was highly esteemed as a gifted scholar by his writings in his twenty years of residence at Valley Center. Tragically he was slain in his store during a holdup in 1907.

VANDEVENTER CREEK. Place-named for a homesteading family whose identity is not known. (Located north from De Luz.)

VIEJAS: Reservation, Mission, Mountain. (Spanish for "old women.") According to local history, an old Indian legend told of a tribal custom of hiding the aged women in this valley whenever the warriors were away at battle. Another local account reported that the Indians of the nineteenth century exiled their aged women to this protected valley to exist – and die – on their own; thereby the tribe was relieved of responsibility to provide food, care, and burial for these aged women. Viejas Mountain and Reservation were designated from this area's place-name. (J.D.)

In 1846 a land grant of 13,000 acres in Alpine district was awarded to Ramon and Leandro Osuna as "Rancho Valle de Las Viejas," an indication that the Spanish or Mexicans in the area had already established this nickname. In 1930 the reservation was established for Indians who were dispossessed by the construction of El Capitan Reservoir. The total area here is 1600 acres. In 1938 the reservation included 80 persons; in 1972 its population was estimated to be 98.

VILLAGER PEAK. Located in extreme northeast part of the county. State Park Ranger Alfred Welcome (Anza-Borrego Desert) reported that two Indian villages once existed here on opposite sides of the elevation. Hence its augmented name.

VISTA. (Spanish for "view.") Originally, this settlement was part of the Buena Vista Rancho, a land grant in 1845 to an Indian neophyte. Homesteaders slowly came into this locale to farm after the gold rush had ended. An attractive settlement developed here in 1890 when the railroad from Oceanside to Escondido was completed, and a local station was established. The railroad line crossed Buena Vista Rancho which had an earlier established depot named "Buena Vista." When a name was required for the new station, "Buena Vista" station was halved: "Buena" for the older station, and "Vista" for the new one. (G.) (See also under BUENA.)

For years Vista consisted of a store, post office, blacksmith shop, railroad station, and a cluster of houses. The settlement grew rapidly once water was brought to this district from Lake Henshaw in 1926.

Climate and soil in the district were especially suitable for cultivation of avocados and wine grapes. When the Delpy Winery was dismantled in 1971, its sign "Jules J. Delpy Corner — Since 1879" was also demolished. (*The Vista Press,* May 30, 1971.)

Language note: *Vista,* a Spanish word for "view," was not frequently designated during Spanish and Mexican occupation. Most place-names that include "vista" are of Yankee designation, its usage having been superlatively popular in San Diego County as a descriptive name for real estate subdivisions. (J.D.) In 1974 Vista ranked ninth in county population.

VISTA DEL MALPAIS. (Spanish for "view of the badlands.") According to Horace Parker, this geographical desert site of erosion and ancient sediments remained unseen and unknown until recently. (p. 23) (See also under FONTS POINT and BORREGO BADLANDS.)

VITA SPRING. Was this spring named by an erudite pioneer of Jamul district bragging about the "life" quality of the water?

VOLCAN MOUNTAIN. (Spanish for "volcano.") This is a mountain range of almost 15 miles in extent, separating San Felipe Valley from Santa Ysabel Valley. Samuel Neason homesteaded a cattle ranch here in 1859. Because its peak suggested a volcano to earlier Spanish or Mexican travelers in the valley, it was named "volcan." The Indian name was "Ha-ha-che-pahg," meaning "place where the water comes down." (J.D.)

WALKER CANYON. Named for George P. Walker, who homesteaded near Boulevard about 1865. The district is mainly desert country, rocky and rough. Because of its inaccessibility and its proximity to the Mexican border, this canyon was believed to have been a frequent hideaway for rustlers, smugglers, desperados, and fugitives from justice. (J.D.)

WARNER SPRINGS. Named for Jonathan Trumbull (Juan Jose) Warner, who arrived in California in 1831, became a Mexican citizen, and eventually controlled and operated almost 45,000 acres of ranch land. His Mexican land grants included Rancho San Jose del Valle (north of the springs) and Rancho Valle de San Jose (south of the springs). These are now known as "Warner's Ranch" and "Warner Springs." Until 1835 the Missions San Diego and San Luis Rey grazed their herds and flocks on these lands. (J.D.)

Warner's ownership and operation of the ranchos coincided with the first southwest expansion of Yankees from the East: they were for early immigrants who came to California via a southern route what Sutter's Fort was for the immigrants who entered California via the central route.

Lt. Emory, chief of the U.S. Topographical Engineers, described his first visit to Warner's Ranch:

> We went over to the place of Warner. A tall man − bottom of the legs − half Californian, half sailor, I thought. When we entered he was seated at breakfast, which probably had put him at his best humor. Quite talkative; said he would

let us have some milk tomorrow morning; and at some inconvenience to himself, sugar and salt. His reception was very courteous; we formed a favorable impression of him.

His house is thatched with tule (cane); divided into two large apartments; with a shed in front before which were stretched out several hides in the process of being dressed for market. Several Indians around and some hired white men. . . .

It (the house) is precisely at the point where the old main road branches, one fork to the town of San Diego, the other to Los Angeles — convenient for the supply of emigrants. He says he will find something to trade with the emigrants as fast as they come. None shall starve. . . .The Indians refer to Warner as Juan Largo (Long John) because of his tall stature.

In 1903 the Indians in Warner Springs were dispossessed and moved to a new reservation of 3400 acres in Pala Valley. One year before this forced removal, Cecilio Blacktooth, chief of the Agua Caliente Indians, made the following eloquent speech to a federal investigating committee to protest the planned removal of the Indians:

We thank you for coming here to talk to us in a way we can understand. It is the first time anyone has done so. You ask us to think what place we like next best to this place where we always live. You see that graveyard over there? There are our fathers and grandfathers. You see that Eagle Nest mountain and that Rabbit-Hole mountain? When God made them He gave us this place. We have always been here. We do not care for any other place. It may be good, but it is not ours. We have always lived here. We would rather die here. Our fathers did. We cannot leave them. Our children born here — how can we go away? If you give us the best place in the world, it is not so good for us as this. My people cannot go anywhere else; they cannot live anywhere else. Here they always live; their people always live here. There is no other place. We ask you to get it for us. If Harvey Downey say he own the place, that is wrong. The Indians always here. We do not go on his land. We stay on ours. Everybody knows this Indian land. These Hot Springs always Indian. We cannot live anywhere else. We were born here and our fathers are buried here. We do not think of any place after this. We want this place and not any other place. There is no other place for us. If you do not buy this place we will go into the mountains like quail and die there, the old people and the women and children. Let the Government be glad and proud. It can kill us. We do not fight. We do what it says. If we cannot live here, we want to go into those mountains and die. We do not want any other home.

The above speech became a part of the Congressional Record — all to no avail. The Supreme Court in 1901 had already ruled that these Indians had no just claim to this land.

WARREN CANYON. Long-time resident Mrs. Vera Warren reported that her husband's grandfather, Edward Boyle Warren, came into Poway district with his family as a homesteader in the 1870s. Born in England and educated as a lawyer, he emigrated to Canada. In 1870 he sold his law books and other possessions in order to raise money for his emigration to San Diego County. Mr. and Mrs. Warren both taught school in Poway district. Mr. Warren also operated a village store and served as postmaster. Their small ranch was considered a showplace in its day because of its design and its gardens.

WEAVER MOUNTAIN. Jim Yarger, long-time resident in San Luis Rey district, recalled that U.S. Weaver farmed grain in Rancho Bernardo area in 1900. About 1919 he homesteaded in the area near Rainbow. Mr. Yarger recalled that Mr. Weaver never revealed the significance of his "U.S." initials.

WELL OF EIGHT ECHOES. An interesting form of folk-name for a well situated south from Agua Caliente Springs. Local history reports that the number of echoes produced by a shout into this well depended on the air volume of the shouter. (H. Parker, p. 60)

150

WEOWLET SPRING. A possible Indian name whose meaning remains unascertained. (Borrego Desert.)

WEST FORK SAN LUIS RIVER. (See under SAN LUIS and SOUTH FORK ALDER CANYON.)

WEST SYCAMORE CANYON. A branch of Sycamore Canyon north from Santee.

WHALE PEAK. State Park Ranger Alfred Welcome (Anza-Borrego Desert) reported that this elongated elevation suggests an outline of a whale. (See also under BALLENA.)

WHELAN LAKE. Miss Ellen Douglas Whelan has resided in Oceanside district for a long time. She reported that her father, John Whelan, was one of a family of 16 children born in Ireland. Fifteen of these sons and daughters (including John) left Ireland to come to America. John Whelan settled in Riverside. The Pico family in Riverside won this lake as the result of a horse race wager, and it became known as Pico's Lake. Becoming interested in ranching at the lake, John Whelan leased the land from the Pico family. Miss Whelan stated that her father preferred to lease land to avoid paying taxes. Years later Miss Whelan purchased the property and established an extensive ranch.

Miss Whelan (who was born in Riverside) claims to be a descendant of the famous Senator Stephen Douglas of Illinois.

WHITE MOUNTAIN. A descriptive place-name for the color-composition of this site in Dulzura district.

WHITE OAK SPRINGS. Apparently named for a species of oak tree at the spring. (Located northeast from San Onofre.)

WILDCAT: Canyon, Spring. Possibly a folk-form of place-name as the result of a wildcat having been encountered or killed. (Located respectively in Barona and Cuyamaca regions.)

WILL VALLEY. Jeff Cook and his three sons, Hiram, George, and Will, settled in Palomar district in the 1880s, coming to California from Texas in a covered wagon. The valley Will chose to homestead was named for him. (C. Wood, p. 55)

WINDMILL: Canyon, Lake. Oceanside historian Ernest Taylor reported that a windmill was placed at a well near this Oceanside site. Apparently it became a landmark in earlier days. (San Luis Rey River district.)

WIRE MOUNTAIN. Located on Camp Pendleton, this site is now occupied by Wire Mountain Marine housing. It apparently was named "Wire Mountain" when the Marine Communications School was first situated here. Its earlier place-name is not known.

WITCH: Settlement, Creek, Mountain. The Indian name for this creek in Santa Ysabel area was "Haguochay," signifying "bewitched water." Local legend long ago reported that an Indian who drank from this stream dropped dead soon afterwards. This incident was believed to have caused the Indians to avoid the creek and its surroundings as a place of misfortune. (J.D.)

John L. McIntyre was the first settler here in 1858. As several Englishmen also settled here, for the next 25 years this locality was regarded as a miniature British colony. By 1886 this sparse settlement had a schoolhouse, blacksmith shop, hotel, and butcher shop.

The mountain and settlement in Santa Ysabel district were named after the creek.

WOLFE WELL. An old Standard Oil well site in Anza-Borrego Desert. Its name origin remains unexplained.

WONDERSTONE WASH. Located in the extreme northeast of the county. State Ranger Alfred Welcome (Anza-Borrego Desert) reported that rhyolite, also known as wonderstone, once existed here in abundance. Hence its present place-name.

> Historical social note:
> In those days quilting and snuff-dipping were the fashion for the ladies. Quilting frames were hung in the living room of every house. A small box of snuff, some pine slivers, and a little water stood on a table. The ladies took a sliver, dipped it in water, then in the snuff, rubbed it around their gums, and left it in their mouth to chew. Grandmother Crouch said it was very enjoyable, far better and less work than the afternoon teas which women now have. *(The San Diego Union,* April 5, 1951, interview with Mrs. Mary Sawday Starr.)

WOODED HILL. A name-designation which is most modest in description, for this mountain has the highest elevation in the county. (Located in Laguna district.)

WOODSON MOUNTAIN. Place-name in Poway area for Dr. Marshall Clay Woodson who homesteaded 320 acres at the mountain base in 1873. The family lived here on their ranch until 1900. Woodson was an early planter of eucalyptus trees, most of which are still standing.

The Warner Indians long ago used this elevated feature for a stopover camp as they journeyed seasonally back and forth from the mountains to the coast. Since the light-colored granite boulders on the slope were visible for miles on a bright night, the Indians designated it as "Mountain of Moonlit Rocks." (J.D.)

WOOD VALLEY. Manifestly, this is either a personal or descriptive place-name, located east of Jamul.

WYNOLA VALLEY. An Indian place-name whose meaning and origin are not known. A bachelor hermit named Spencer settled in Santa Ysabel region in the 1860s, and this site was referred to as "Spencer's Valley." A town meeting in 1888 applied for a post office under that name, but it was rejected, as Washington reported such a place-name already existed. School teacher W.A. Sickler suggested the Indian name of "Wynola," which its citizens agreed to accept. (J.D., Ha.)

YAQUI: Flat, Meadows, Pass, Ridge, Well. To wildlife, desert dwellers, travelers, and wagon freighters, this site of water was often of survival significance. It is located close to the once much-traveled, rough Grapevine Canyon road in San Felipe Valley. The well also is an historical artifact of a persistent desert legend of a secret gold mine.

Researcher Marion Beckler reported that the well was named for the two Yaqui Indians who made it usable while in the employ of the owner of the famous Ball Freighter Company. ("Yaqui Well," *San Diego Historical Society Quarterly,* Vol. 9, No. 4, pp. 49-50)

Researcher Philip Bailey reported the legend that the well was named for a Yaqui Indian who lived nearby. He was a sheepherder in Yaqui Pass who had a mysterious source of gold. Efforts of desert men who stalked the roamings of the Yaqui sheepherder to discover his secret gold source were to no avail. *(Golden Mirages,* p. 90)

YUCCA VALLEY. A descriptive place-name after the abundance of these liliaceous plants at this site located northeast from Warner Springs. The yucca's fruit and flowers were often part of the Indians' diet. A spiked variety of yucca was also designated as "Spanish bayonet."

YUIMA: Creek, Indian Reservation. Long-time resident Marcus Golsh, of Indian descent, reported that "Yuima" translates as "place near the sight of snow." It is located in Pauma Valley district.

Golsh reported that the Yuima Indian Reservation is of small acreage, with few Indians as residents. He did not know whether the creek or the reservation was first named "Yuima."

ZUNIGA POINT. Captain George Vancouver named this site in 1793 in honor of Lt. Jose de Zuniga, commandant of San Diego Presidio. Vancouver referred to San Diego Presidio as "least of the California establishments." (W.D.)

Bibliography

BASIC SOURCES
(listed in order of importance)

Davidson, John. "San Diego Place Names." Eighteen scrapbooks of San Diego weekly newspaper columns, 1934-1943, alphabetically indexed. San Diego Historical Society. Serra Museum Library.

Davidson, John. *San Diego County Place Names 1934-1936.* 3 vol. California Room, San Diego Public Library.

Davidson, John. *Some Place Names in San Diego County, 1934-1939.* 3 vol. California Room, San Diego Public Library.

Davidson, Winifred S. "San Diego Names." Clippings from San Diego newspapers in "Place Names" Vertical File, San Diego Historical Society, Serra Museum Library.

Davidson, Winifred. *San Diego Names.* 1 vol. Compiled by The California Room, San Diego Public Library, 1966. 55 numbered leaves.

Hunzicker, Lena B. Three unpublished notebooks of San Diego County Place Names, undated. San Diego Historical Society, Serra Museum Library.

Gudde, Erwin G. *California Place Names.* Berkeley: University of California Press, 1967. Second edition, third printing.

Federal Writers' Project, compiled by Bawden. "Bawden Field Notes." Works Progress Administration, San Diego Historical Society, Serra Museum Library.

Hanna, Phil Townsend. *The Dictionary of California Land Names.* Los Angeles: Automobile Club of Southern California, 1951.

The above basic sources are acknowledged in the text as follows:
J.D.   John Davidson
W.D.   Winifred Davidson
Hu.   Lena B. Hunzicker
G.   Erwin G. Gudde
B.   Federal Writers' Project, Bawden
Ha.   Phil Townsend Hanna

157

ADDITIONAL SOURCES

Bailey, Philip A. *Golden Mirages.* New York: Macmillan Co., 1940.

Barrows, David P. *The Ethno-Botany of the Coahuilla Indians of Southern California.* Chicago: The University of Chicago Press, 1900.

Beckler, Marion. "Yaqui Well." *Journal of San Diego History.* San Diego Historical Society. Vol. IX, No. 4, 1964, pp. 49-50.

Brackett, R.W. *The History of San Diego County Ranchos.* Sponsored by the San Diego Historical Society. San Diego: Union Title Insurance Co., 1960.

Chase, Joseph Smeaton. *California Desert Trails.* Boston and New York: Houghton Mifflin Co., 1919.

Davis, Abel M. *Valley Center, California, From The Memoirs of Abel Davis.* Valley Center: 1955.

Dumke, Glenn S. *The Boom of the Eighties in Southern California.* San Marino: Huntington Library, 1944.

Emory, Lt. Col. W.H. *Notes of a Military Reconnaissance....* 30th Cong., 1st Sess., House Exec. Doc. No. 41. Washington, D.C., 1848. San Diego Historical Society, Serra Museum Library.

Federal Writers' Project. "Story of the Indians of San Diego County." Manuscript. San Diego Historical Society, Serra Museum Library.

Gray, Don. W. "Mountain Springs Grade," *California Highways and Public Works.* Jan.-Feb. 1964, pp. 43-47.

Greene, Nellie B. "History of California." Scrapbook I. San Diego Historical Society, Serra Museum Library.

Guinn, J.M. *A History of California and an Extended History of its Southern Coast Counties....* Los Angeles: Historic Record Co., 1907. 2 vols.

Gunn, Douglas. *Picturesque San Diego.* Chicago: Knight & Leonard Co., 1887.

Hayes, Benjamin I. *Pioneer Notes from the Diaries of Judge Benjamin Hayes,* 1849-1875. Edited and published by Marjorie Tisdale Wolcott. Los Angeles: McBride Printing Co., 1929.

Hensley, Herbert C. "Memoirs of Herbert C. Hensley." Manuscript, 1949-1952. Vol. II. San Diego Historical Society, Serra Museum Library.

History of Carlsbad, compiled by Friends of the Library of Carlsbad, California, 1961.

Jackson, Helen Hunt. *A Century of Dishonor.* Boston: Roberts Brothers, 1886.

Jackson, Helen Hunt. "The Present Condition of Mission Indians in Southern California." Indian box file. San Diego Historical Society, Serra Museum Library.

Jasper, James A. "Picturesque Lakeside," *The Silver Gate,* Jan. 1900, p. 9.

Johnson, Mary Elizabeth. *Indian Legends of the Cuyamaca Mountains.* San Diego: Printed by Frye & Smith, 1914.

Lee, Bob. *Lost Mines and Buried Treasure of San Diego.* Ramona, California: Ballena Press, 1973.

McCain, Ella. "Memories of the Early Settlements, Dulzura, Potrero, and Campo." Manuscript, 1955. San Diego Historical Society, Serra Museum Library.

McGrew, Clarence A. *City of San Diego and San Diego County.* Chicago and New York: American Historical Society, 1922. 2 vols.

Parker, Horace. *Anza-Borrego Desert Guide Book; Southern California's Last Frontier.* Maps by Jack P. Welch. Balboa Island, California: Paisano Press, 1969.

Reed, Lester. *Old Time Cattlemen and Other Pioneers of the Anza-Borrego Area.* Palm Desert, California: Desert Printers, 1963.

Robinson, William W. *Land in California.* Berkeley: University of California Press, 1948.

Rush, Philip Scott. *Some Old Ranchos and Adobes.* San Diego: Neyenesch Printers, 1964.

Ryan, Frances and Lewis. *Early Days in Escondido.* Escondido: Privately published, 1970.

Sanchez, Nellie Van de Grift. *Spanish and Indian Place Names of California.* San Francisco: A.M. Robertson, 1922.

Schmid, Dorothy Clark. *Pioneering in Dulzura.* San Diego: Robert R. Knapp, 1963.

Scott, E.B. "Biographical Sketches and Early History of Encinitas 1882-1891." Manuscript. San Diego Historical Society, Serra Museum Library.

Smythe, William E. *History of San Diego, 1542-1908.* San Diego: The History Company, 1908. 2 vol.

Sparkman, Philip Stedman. "The Culture of the Luiseño Indians." *University of California Publications in American Archaeology and Ethnology,* Vol. 8, No. 4. Berkeley: The University Press, 1908.

Stanford, Leland G. "San Diego's Eucalyptus Bubble," *Journal of San Diego History,* Vol. XVI, No. 4. San Diego, 1970, pp. 11-14.

Stewart, George R. *Names on the Land.* Boston: Houghton Mifflin Co., 1958.

Summers, June Nay. *Buenos Dias, Tecate.* Yuma, Arizona: Southwest Printers, 1972.

Sweeny, Thomas William. *Journal of Lt. Thomas W. Sweeny 1849-1853.* Edited by Arthur Woodward. Los Angeles: Westernlore Press, 1956.

Union Title Trust Topics, "Rancho Santa Fe." San Diego: April-May, 1947, pp. 2-7.

Van Dyke, T.S. *The City and County of San Diego.* San Diego: Leberthon & Taylor, 1888.

Witty, Robert M. and Neil Morgan. *Marines of the Margarita.* San Diego: Frye & Smith, Ltd., 1970.

Wood, Catherine M. *Palomar from tepee to telescope.* San Diego: Frye & Smith, Ltd., 1937.

Pronunciation Guide

Agua Caliente   *AH-wah-kahl-YEN-tay*
Agua Hedionda   *AH-wah-ay-DYOHN-dah*
Agua Tibia   *AH-wah-TEE-byah*
Aguanga   *ah-WAHNG-gah*
Aliso   *ah-LEE-soh*
Anahuac   *AH-nah-hwak*
Arroyo Seco   *ahr-ROY-oh-SAY-koh*
Arroyo Tapiado   *ahr-ROY-oh-tah-PYAH-doh*
Ballena   *bah-YAY-nah*
Batequitos   *bah-tay-KEE-tohss*
Bisnaga   *beess-NAH-gah*
Bonita   *boh-NEE-tah*
Borrego   *bor-RAY-goh*
Buena   *BWAY-nah*
Calavera   *kah-lah-VAIR-ah*
Cañada   *kah-NYAH-dah*
Capitan   *kah-pee-TAHN*
Carrizo   *kahr-REE-zoh*
Conejos   *koh-NAY-hohss*
Cuyamaca   *kwee-ah-MAH-kah*
Cuyapaipa   *kwee-ah-PIE-pah*
Deguynos   *day-GEEN-ohss*
De Luz   *day-LOOSE*
Dos Cabezas   *dohss-kah-BAY-sahs*
Durasnitos   *due-rahs-NEE-tohs*
El Cajon   *ell-kah-HOHN*

Guajome *why-HOH-may*
Guatay *WHAT-eye*
Guejito *way-HEE-toh*
Hapaha *HAH-pah-hah*
Jacumba *hah-KOOM-bah*
Jamacha *HAH-ma-shah*
Jamul *hah-MOOL*
Japatul *HAH-pah-tool*
La Jolla *lah-HOY-yah*
Leucadia *loo-KAY-dee-ah*
Los Guijarros *lohs-gee-HAHR-rohss*
Mataqual *MAH-tah-hwal*
Mateo *mah-TAY-oh*
Mesa Grande *MAY-sah-GRAHN-day*
Monserate *MOHN-sair-aht*
Morena *moh-RAY-nah*
Olivenhain *oh-LEEV-en-hine*
Olla *OY-yah*
Onofre *oh-NOH-fray*
Oriflamme *OR-ee-flahm*
Otay *OH-tie*
Pala *PAH-lah*
Palo Verde *PAH-loh-VAIR-day*
Pauma *PAW-mah*
Peñasquitos *payn-yahss-KEE-tohss*
Piños *PEEN-yohss*
Poway *POW-eye*
San Dieguito *sahn-dyay-GEE-toh*
San Elijo *sahn-ay-LEE-ho*
San Ysidro *sahn-ee-SEE-droh*
Tecate *tay-KAH-tay*
Trujillo *true-HEE-yoh*
Tules *TOO-lays*
Un Gallo *oohn-GAH-yoh*
Viejas *VYAY-hahss*
Yuima *you-EE-mah*

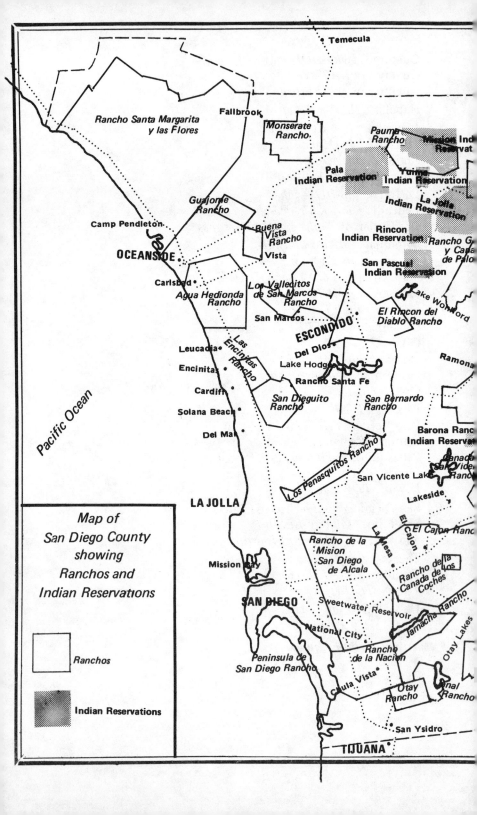

Map of
San Diego County
showing
Ranchos and
Indian Reservations

Ranchos

Indian Reservations

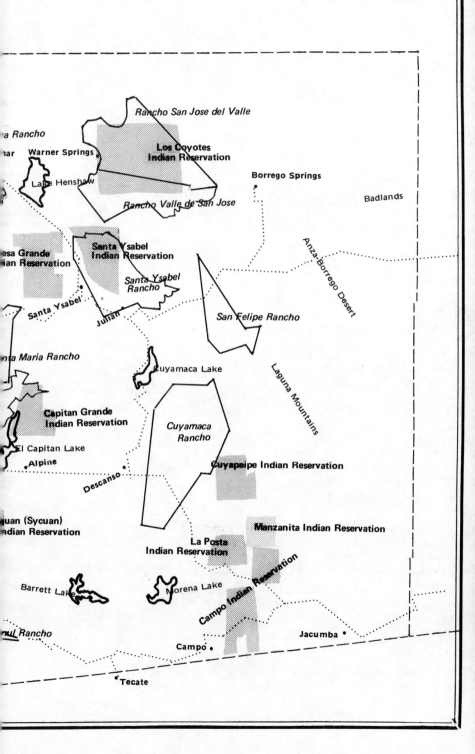

Rancho San Jose del Valle

Los Coyotes Indian Reservation

a Rancho

Warner Springs

har

Lake Henshaw

Borrego Springs

Badlands

Rancho Valle de San Jose

Santa Ysabel Indian Reservation

esa Grande ian Reservation

Santa Ysabel Rancho

Santa Ysabel

Julian

San Felipe Rancho

Anza-Borrego Desert

nta Maria Rancho

Cuyamaca Lake

Laguna Mountains

Capitan Grande Indian Reservation

Cuyamaca Rancho

El Capitan Lake

Alpine

Cuyapaipe Indian Reservation

Descanso

Manzanita Indian Reservation

quan (Sycuan) ndian Reservation

La Posta Indian Reservation

Barrett Lake

Morena Lake

Campo Indian Reservation

nul Rancho

Jacumba

Campo

Tecate